American Society and Popular Culture

This study was financially supported by Initiative for College of Humanities' Research and Education of National Research Foundation of Korea, 2017

American Society and Popular Culture

by

Robert Grotjohn

Chonnam National University PRESS

the Title of

American Society and Popular Culture

First published June 2017
Written by Robert Grotjohn (Ph.D), Chonnam National University
Publisher: Byung-Seok Jeong
ISBN 978-89-6849-413-0 (93300)
Price: 12,000 Won

Published by Chonnam National University Press,
77 Yongbong-ro, Bukgu, Gwangju,
Republic of Korea, 61186
Tel: 82-62-530-0571/3, Fax: 82-62-530-0579

Printed and bound in the Republic of Korea

CIP No : CIP2017015361

Acknowledgements

The publication of this book was made possible with the financial support of the National Research Foundation of Korea through a CORE (Initiative for College of Humanities' Research and Education) grant from the College of Humanities, Chonnam National University.

This book has developed as a natural outgrowth of my teaching. For the opportunity to "earn my chops" as a teacher, I have to thank the administrators, professors, and, most importantly, the students of Mary Baldwin College (now University), where I taught for seventeen years before returning to South Korea and Chonnam National University in 2010. For the opportunity to return, I thank the administration of Chonnam University, and, especially, my colleagues in the Department of English Language and Literature. Your warm welcome and consistent support for this foreigner have made me feel at home in Gwangju. I can never repay your collegial generosity and friendship.

At Chonnam University, it has been my good fortune to teach a class in American Society and Popular Culture, and the teaching topics and materials for that class have gradually developed into the text that follows. I have to thank every student who ever took the class for showing me what works in the class, and what does not. Without your enthusiasm and good humor, I would never have had the motivation to complete this textbook.

I want to thank Chonnam University and its College of Humanities for the sabbatical time that permitted the completion of this book, and, again, Mary Baldwin University for welcoming me back to Virginia and giving me research time and space as a visiting faculty member during that sabbatical.

Preface

This book is written specifically for the Korean college classroom, so there will be many connections to contemporary Korea. Most university classrooms in Korea have a good number of international students, and the book is written with that fact in mind. I hope that the ideas here can serve to inspire many cross-cultural discussions between students from many different countries.

I ask students to engage in critical thinking about popular culture as texts that reflect U.S. American beliefs and values; therefore, much of the first six chapters establishes a foundation for those beliefs and values at the same time as it begins the practice of critical engagement with cultural texts such as popular songs. Those U.S. values are common but not universal, and they often conflict.

The ultimate goal is to make students better consumers of popular culture, to help them understand how popular culture influences how we think and what we value, to help them to become more critically and analytically engaged with their own lives in society. This approach toward popular culture responds to that ageless Socratic dictum to "know yourself."

Interspersed throughout the chapters are brief interludes titled "QUESTION." Not all of these are formed as questions, but all are brief pauses for thought in the midst of the reading. For some of those questions, I have suggested answers. Readers should always try to answer the questions for themselves before moving on to my answers. For other questions, readers will have to come up with answers for themselves.

A section titled "FOR FURTHER CONSIDERATION" concludes each chapter. These sections introduce topics, websites, songs, and various other popular culture texts. Students can use those topics and texts to explore the ideas developed in the chapter. Most of these further considerations require somewhat deeper thought than the questions interspersed through the reading. These considerations can be used for class discussions, group presentations, writing topics, or in other creative ways. When I teach the class, I often ask students to submit regular journal-type responses on topics and texts from the further considerations. Those do not have to be formal writing assignments but can be a way for students to practice writing complex ideas in English without much pressure for grammatical and idiomatic perfection.

If students answer the questions and/or address the topics for further consideration in class discussion, it is helpful for students to consider their responses in small groups of three to five students. If a class has many international students, I suggest placing at least one international student in each group. That way, people in the groups will need to have discussions in English. Since many students will take this class as a way to improve their English, even groups with only Korean students should try to speak in English at all times. Since English-language ability may vary widely among the students, I often ask those Korean students with high-level ability to assist those of lower-level ability by explaining concepts in Korean, as much as time allows.

I point students to many websites to enhance their learning experience. The internet is an essential aspect of today's popular culture. The URL addresses were all current when I wrote the text, but sometimes they change, and students might have to use a search engine to find some of the resources.

Instructors will have to pick and choose which chapters or parts of chapters that will work best for their own interests and teaching styles. I have used the material presented in each of the chapters, but I have never used all of it in a single semester. For instance, I do very little with March Madness when I teach the class in the Fall, but I spend more time in the Spring because the students can actively participate in following the tournament results.

I could have included other topics, or given greater emphasis to topics such as television or social media, which I address only in passing. Conversely, one could spend an entire semester on a small fraction of the material here. I can imagine a course that focuses exclusively on sports, or on music, or on film. In a course like this, an instructor should follow his or her own inclinations to engage students in the primary goal of the course, developing the ability to think critically about the world around us.

Besides emphasizing critical thinking, I return to the connections between past and present that are evident in the study and enjoyment of popular culture. I hope the students will use those connections to better understand themselves not just as consumers of the currently popular but as historical actors.

Finally, I hope that this course is interesting, even fun. The culture addressed in this book is popular because it interests many people. It brings them pleasure that I hope can be deepened through study and through the greater understanding that comes from that study.

Contents

Topic 1

Who Is an American?

In order to consider who Americans are, we should be sure we know where America is located. Where is America on this map?

Some people might be tempted to choose just these parts of the map:

That would be incorrect. Those places are the *United States of* America only. Every place on the map is America: North America, Central America, South America, and the Caribbean are all parts of America, which is a pair of continents not just one country. The country called 미국 (*miguk*) is not all of America. It is one among many countries on the two continents of America. Often, when someone uses the word "America," they are referring to the U.S.A., and that will be the case in this book at times, but it is important to keep in mind that the U.S.A. is not all of America. Thus, what or who an American is can be a complicated question.

To consider some complications, look at this photo of me:

Do I look like a Korean, or do I look like an American? The answer to that is probably pretty obvious.

Now, think about your college classes in Korea.

Q : How many students in your classes look like Americans?

Before I give my answer to that last question, I would like to tell a story. Before, I tell the story, however, I would like you to think of American geography again because that geography is important to my story.

Q : What are some of the most famous cities in the U.S.? See if you can locate them on a map.

Q : What is the capital of the U.S., the city with the White House, where the President and his family live, and the Capitol Building, where the Senate and the House of Representatives meet to enact laws?

That city is, of course, Washington, D.C. Washington lies between two states, Maryland to the northeast and Virginia to the southwest. In the area known as Northern Virginia is a suburb of Washington named Annandale, a city with a large Korean American population.

Once, a few years ago, when I lived in Virginia, I looked on the internet and found some Korean restaurants in Annandale. One day, when I was in Annandale with a Korean friend, we drove to one of the restaurants. Across the highway from the restaurant was a video-rental store, the 안방 비디오실 (*Anbang Videoshil*).

By the way, do you know what the 안방 (*anbang*) is? I am not asking about the contemporary meaning but about the traditional meaning from the Joseon Dynasty. In that meaning, the *anbang* is the women's living space: "As the center of activity space for women, it served the multiple functions of dwelling, dining, reception, and housework during the daytime and sleeping at night."[1)]

Q : Given the name of the store, what kind of movies and TV programs do you think were available to rent? (Those forms of entertainment are, of course, significant forms of *popular culture*.)

If you answered soap operas and "chick flicks," you would be correct. A chick flick is a film that appeals to women: "chick" is a term for young women, derived from the Spanish *chiquita*—it is often considered a derogatory, sexist term, and you probably should not use it because it may offend some people. The word "flick" is a slang term for movies. The films and programs available at the 안방 비디오실 (*Anbang Videoshil*) were created for a primarily female audience.

1) Yoon, Sunyoung and Kyungran Choi, "Comparative Study on Korean and Chinese Housing Based on Cultural Patterns - From the 15th Century to the Present," idemployee.id.tue.nl/g.w.m.rauterberg/conferences/cd_donotopen/adc/final_paper/452.pdf.

One thing we can note in this context is that pop culture changes quickly. The 안방 비디오실 (*Anbang Videoshil*) had many VHS (Video Home System) tapes; in July 2016, the very last VCR (Video Cassette Recorder) machines were manufactured. Videos were replaced by DVDs (Digital Video Discs), and DVDs have been replaced by downloading and live streaming as a way of watching movies without going to a movie theater. Indeed, it is hard to find a video store anymore, maybe it is even impossible, since online services have taken over video distribution. Obviously, technology has helped to change popular culture and the way we consume it.

But back to my story. My Korean friend and I went into the 안방 비디오실 (*Anbang Videoshil*) to ask about the Korean restaurant across the highway. My Korean friend asked the clerk in Korean if the restaurant was a good place to eat. The clerk replied, "외국놈 좋아하는데요. . ." (*weyguknom joahaneundaeyo*: Well, foreigners like it), implying, of course, that a Korean who knows the difference between good Korean food and bad Korean food would not enjoy the restaurant very much. Implying also, I think, that I might like it, since I was a "foreigner."

My Korean-language skills are not great, but I do know that it is not very polite to refer to someone standing in front of you with the word "놈" (*nom*), which is often considered a derogatory term to use of another person. In order to indicate to the woman working at the store that

I realized I had the opportunity to be offended, I responded in my not-very-good Korean, "그저 그래요?" (*geujeo geuraeyo*: only so-so?). The clerk was surprised and made sure that she referred to "외국사람" (*weyguksaram*: foreign people) for the rest of our brief conversation, since the word 사람 (*saram*) is more polite than 놈 (*nom*). In fact, she became extremely helpful and showed us how to get to the best nearby Korean restaurant, one that even Koreans liked.

That is my story.

Q : What are your reactions to the story? What do you think is strange about the clerk's response to my friend's inquiry about the restaurant?

Some people might see the woman as rude because she called me *weygu**knom*** rather than the more polite *weygu**ksaram***, but the former is fairly common among Koreans and probably was not intended to make me feel bad. She may not even have considered the language impolite until she heard my response. For her, it may have just been what she was used to saying and hearing. It was not a strange response, and it was not one that offended me, although it was fun to let her know that I understood.

Perhaps some might see it as strange, or at least ironic, that an immigrant (the clerk) would call someone who was born and raised in the U.S. (me) a "foreigner." It might seem especially strange since the story takes place just outside the capital of the U.S., the political center of the country in which I was born – in my country. Who was the foreigner in the story? Some people might say that she was the foreigner. What business did she have calling *me* a foreigner in my own country?

Those are two possible responses to my story. I prefer a third way to understand it: I would say that there were ***no*** foreigners in the story. The clerk in the video store was also an American, even though she spoke Korean and probably was born in Korea. America is a country with great ethnic and racial *diversity*. That *diversity* is the first principle of American culture and society that I want to emphasize. Yes, the U.S. is my country, but it was hers as well.

And that brings me back to the question that preceded the story: How many students in your Korean classrooms look like Americans?

My answer is that every single student in those classrooms looks like an American. Americans are not just "Anglo-Saxon" like me. For some people, that is the stereotype of the American, but *stereotypes* are not reality. Americans come in many colors, creeds, and religions. Some of them speak Korean as a first language and refer to non-Koreans as 외국사람 (*weyguksaram*).

I suppose I do not look very Korean, but ***everyone*** in a Korean classroom looks like he or she could be an American. The U.S. is, for the great majority of its people, a nation of immigrants or of people descended from immigrants. No one in the U.S. who does not have Native American heritage can trace their *American* family line back before the 16th century, and most people cannot trace it even that far. My own ancestors came from Germany in the middle to late 19th century. My grandfather, who was a third-generation German-American, grew up in a German-speaking home, and he never lost his German accent. He was an American whose first language was not English, just like the woman in the *Anbang Videoshil* is American.

Americans are a diverse people, and that *diversity* is embraced with pride by many Americans. Even the word "foreigner" is sometimes considered too exclusionary. Most colleges and universities no longer have foreign students; they have international students. Using the word "international" rather than the word "foreign" implies a more inclusive attitude. Foreigners are different, strange, outsiders. International students may have differences, but they are not strange and they are not considered outsiders.

Q : Why are Native Americans called "Indians"?[2)]

Not every American shares an open perspective on American diversity, however. Some people insist only those who are born in the U.S. and speak English are "real"

2) Because Christopher Columbus thought he had landed in India in 1492.

Americans. Some of those people might even think that only white people are fully "American." Indeed Americans of Asian ancestry (Asian Americans), who might be fourth- or fifth-generation Americans, often report that some people express surprise when they speak English clearly and with no foreign accent.

Here are just a few examples of Americans who reject diversity in language.

- A Philadelphia food stand owner posted these two signs next to one another: "This is America. When ordering 'Speak English.'" and "Management Reserves the Right to Refuse Service." That is, if customers do not speak English, the owner may refuse to serve them.[3)]
- Sometimes, a person might see bumper stickers and signs with slogans like "I Want You to Speak English or Get Out" and "Welcome to America, Now Speak English" and "Your in America, Speak English."[4)]

The last one ("Your in America, Speak English") shows that the writer himself cannot use English correctly. The writer uses "Your" when the correct word is "You're," the contraction for "You are." It is ironic that the writer wants

3) "Philly Officials Warn Eatery for English-only Sign," *NBC News* 12 June 2006. www.nbcnews.com/id/13272368/ns/us_news-life/t/philly-officials-warn-eatery-english-only-sign/#.WItGa_krLIU

4) Bumper stickers found at zazzle.com/speak+english+bumperstickers.

others to use English when the writer cannot use it properly.

Here are other signs with the same kind of irony.

Q : What are the errors in the sentences below?

- A previous mayor of Crestwood, Illinois, once posted a sign that read: "English is Our Language. No Excetions. Learn it."
- "This is America and our only Langogueage is English"
- "Respect are country, speak English"[5)]

The rejection of linguistic diversity has its roots in a rejection of racial and ethnic diversity that is an unpleasant aspect of American history and of parts of contemporary American society. Through much of American history, there were separate water fountains for white and black people. Often, black people could not go to the same restaurants, hotels, and schools as white people, and they were not permitted to sit next to white people in movie theaters. For many years, black people were forced by law to sit in the back of public buses.

Not only black people suffered from racial *discrimination.*

5) The errors: "Exceptions" not "Ecxetions"; "Language" not "Langoguage"; "our" not "are." All of these are from "10 Ironic 'Speak English' Signs," *Huffington Post*, 22 September 2012, huffingtonpost.com/2012/09/22/13-ironic-speak-english-signs_n_1906008.html.

Here are what was written on a few signs in America's past.

- We serve whites only. No Spanish or Mexicans.[6)]
- Japs keep moving. This is a white man's neighborhood.[7)]
- This park was given for white people only. Mexicans and Negroes stay out.[8)]

Fortunately, since the Civil Rights Movement of the 1950s and 1960s, such racial discrimination has been ruled illegal. There may still be too many racial problems in the U.S., but overt discrimination is not generally accepted or legal in the 21st century.

FOR FURTHER CONSIDERATION

Compare diversity in Korea or some other country with diversity in the U.S. as discussed in this chapter. You may use your own country if you are an international student from some country other than the U.S. Try to use specific examples in your comparison.

---

6) Cynthia E. Orozo, *No Mexicans, Women, or Dogs Allowed: The Rise of the Mexican American Civil Rights Movement* (University of Texas Press, 2006), 55.

7) "A More Perfect Union: Japanese Americans and the U.S. Constitution" at *The National Museum of American History* website: amhistory.si.edu/perfectunion/collection/image.asp?ID=411.

8) Stephen Bender, *Mea Culpa: Lessons on Law and Regret from U.S. History* (New York University Press, 2015), 128.

Topic 2

Why Study Pop Culture?

WHAT IS CULTURE? Two 19th-Century Views

The first view of culture given below comes from Matthew Arnold (1822-1888), a 19th-century British writer. He defines culture as "high culture," and he believes that what we now call popular culture has no value. Moreover, he believes that America has no real culture. Arnold has a lot to say about culture in his 1882 book, *Culture and Anarchy*.[1] He defines "culture" as "a pursuit of our total perfection by means of getting to know, on all the matters which most concern us, the best which has been thought and said in the world": for emphasis, I will repeat, "the best which has been thought and said in the world." In distinguishing the "best" from the rest, Arnold is anti-egalitarian in his sympathies. In a famous phrase, he signifies high culture as "sweetness and light."

Arnold "conceive[s] of true human perfection as a *harmonious* perfection, developing all sides of our humanity; and as a general perfection, developing all parts of our society." Here, he seems to have one thing in common with contemporary understanding of popular culture: culture

1) I have used an online copy that can be found at the University of Toronto Library website: library.utoronto.ca/utel/nonfiction_u/arnoldm_ca/ca_ch-1.html.

reveals something about our society. He does not have much respect for American culture, insisting that "America, that chosen home of newspapers and politics, is without general intelligence, . . . that in the things of the mind, and in culture and totality, America, instead of surpassing us all, falls short." In mentioning those newspapers and politics, he refers to the popular culture of the day, and he dismisses it contemptuously. Common people read newspapers instead of great literature; common people get excited about the conflicts in popular democracy. Superior people ignore those common pursuits, according to Arnold.

He dismisses the American university as working from a "misconception of what culture truly is, and to be calculated to produce miners, or engineers, or architects, not sweetness and light." He insists that "a true conception of culture is . . . just what America fails in." He finds America's weakness to be a lack of intelligence: "It is not fatal to Americans to have no religious establishments and no effective centres of high culture; but it is fatal to them to be told by their flatterers, and to believe, that they are the most intelligent people in the whole world, when of intelligence, in the true and fruitful sense of the word, they even singularly, as we have seen, come short."

Quite a different view of American culture is given by Walt Whitman at about the same time. Whitman (1819-1892) is considered America's first great poet, and he attributed American greatness to the energy of the common people. We can see him celebrate those common people, the people that Arnold sees with contempt, in this poem called "I Hear America Singing," which I have taken from the online *Walt Whitman Archive.*[2)]

> I hear America singing, the varied carols I hear,
>
> Those of mechanics, each one singing his as it should be blithe and strong,
>
> The carpenter singing his as he measures his plank or beam,
>
> The mason singing his as he makes ready for work, or leaves off work,
>
> The boatman singing what belongs to him in his boat, the deckhand singing on the steamboat deck,
>
> The shoemaker singing as he sits on his bench, the hatter singing as he stands,
>
> The wood-cutter's song, the ploughboy's on his way in the morning, or at noon intermission or at sundown,
>
> The delicious singing of the mother, or of the young wife at work, or of the girl sewing or washing,
>
> Each singing what belongs to him or her and to none else,
>
> The day what belongs to the day—at night the party

2) whitmanarchive.org/published/LG/1891/poems/19.

of young fellows, robust, friendly,
Singing with open mouths their strong melodious songs.

Q : What kinds of people does Whitman hear "singing"?
How does his idea of important "culture" differ from Arnold's?
Which writer is closest to the idea of "popular" culture?
What are Whitman's American characteristics?

More recently, Michael Petracca and Madeleine Sorapure identify various types of culture.[3] They consider the anthropological sense of culture, which they define as "the distinct practices, artifacts, institutions, customs, and values of a particular social group." They identify high culture, or just "culture" to some, which includes "artifacts traditionally considered worthy of study by . . . educated people." The appreciation of high culture shows "refinement and intellectual superiority" according to its proponents. This is the culture of refined aesthetics that was promoted by Matthew Arnold. One might say of very sophisticated people who know a lot about art and classical music and the great works of literature, "She is a very cultured person."

3) *Common Culture* 5th ed. (Pearson-Prentice Hall, 2007), 2-6.

Folk culture is defined as those things "created by a specific community or ethnic group" that are "generally transmitted through oral communication." Folk culture puts a "high value on tradition." Mass culture is defined as "information we receive through print and electronic media." Mass culture reaches many people through the same media. This is very close to popular culture, and pop culture would not exist in its present form without this technological distribution. Not *all* popular culture is delivered and developed through the mass media, however.

They define subculture as a "specific segment of society outside the core of dominant cultures." Some examples are minority groups, artists, homosexuals, lawyers, teenagers, and b-boys. Counterculture is defined as being against the dominant social order. "Counter" means "against" and can be demonstrated by these opposing pairs: indie music vs. pop music; indie film vs. Hollywood film; hippies of the 60s vs. the "mainstream." Countercultures show "a desire to resist the pressures . . . to conform to a common culture."

Finally, they define popular culture (or just pop culture), the main subject of this book, as that which "represents the elements of everyday life, the artifacts and institutions shared by a society, and a body of common knowledge"; "the shared knowledge and practices of a specific group at a specific time"; it "reflects and influences people's way of life," and it is "transitory, subject to change, and often an initiator of change." As Petracca and Sorapure remind us, "popular" means "of the people." How it gets to be "of the people," how it gets to belong to the people, is a matter of frequent debate.

Carl R. Weinberg, in an essay titled "Learning from Popular Culture," identifies the key positions in this debate, the view that pop culture comes from the top down and is controlled by the media industry, and the view that pop culture comes from the "grassroots," the ordinary people.[4)]

> "Popular culture" is a deceptively simple phrase. Its meaning, at first glance, seems self-evident: culture that is widely popular, like singer Lady Gaga, the movie *Avatar*, and the television show *American Idol*. On deeper examination, though, the plot thickens. Are these forms of amusement popular because they spring from the authentic interests, fears, and desires of the people? Or are they manufactured to create, deepen, and play upon (and prey upon) those wells of emotion? Are they created, in any realistic sense, by ordinary people or are they, rather, created for them by powerful corporate elites looking to rake in profits and distract the majority from more potentially subversive concerns? Or, is it possible that popular culture is a kind of "contested terrain" in which the interests and perspectives of various social groups contend for dominance? . . .
>
> Whichever perspective on popular culture seems

4) Carl R. Weinberg, "Learning from Popular Culture," *OAH Magazine of History* 24.2 (2010): 3.

> most persuasive, it is hard to deny the subject's appeal. While students usually enter a history classroom ignorant of a variety of topics, popular culture is intensely familiar to them. It offers a wealth of bridges between the past and present.

In the later pages of this book, we will consider both the contested terrain of pop culture's origins and the bridges between past and present that it offers. While Petracca and Sorapure rightly note that pop culture is "transitory," temporary, those connections to the past show us how we have developed.

Q : What do *you* think?

Does popular culture "spring from the authentic interests, fears, and desires of the people"? Is it created "by ordinary people"?

Is popular culture "manufactured . . . by powerful corporate elites looking to rake in profits"?

Is popular culture "contested terrain"?

What examples can you use to support your opinion?

Whatever the origin of popular culture, grassroots, top-down, or some combination of them, studying it helps us to understand our world and ourselves. Petracca and

Sorapure explain the importance of popular culture in this way: "We should examine and analyze pop culture, then, in order to assess—and sometimes resist—its influence."

The influences of American popular culture make it important that people from other countries consider their own worlds more critically as well. As LeRoy Ashby writes, "popular culture has become the nation's (the U.S.'s) leading export."[5] Ashby suggests a reason that we sometime might want to resist the attractions of popular culture: a "central ingredient of the entertainment economy is not only the production of amusements, but also the shaping of lifestyles and values built around consumerism."

Ⓠ : Consider the pros and cons of "lifestyles and values built around consumerism."

FOR FURTHER CONSIDERATION

Find the online article by Ashley Lutz in *Business Insider*: "These 6 Corporations Control 90% of the Media in America." What does that tell you about who produces popular culture? About consumerism and popular culture?[6]

---

5) LeRoy Ashby, "Not Necessarily Swill Time: Popular Culture and American History," *OAH Magazine of History* 24.2 (2010): 7-9.

6) businessinsider.com/these-6-corporations-control-90-of-the-media-in-america-2012-6. For other perspectives on this topic, see: "Concentration of Media Ownership," *Slide Share* at slideshare.net/shubhamnag3/concentration-of-media-ownership-15621788; "Who Owns the Media?" *Freepress* at freepress.net/ownership/chart; "Save the Internet" at

Some Pop Culture Websites: Look at several of these websites that seem interesting to you and briefly report on them to the class or in writing. Your instructor might assign specific sites to individuals or groups.

- *American Popular Culture*: americanpopularculture.com/home.htm.
- *Americana: The Journal of American Popular Culture*: americanpopularculture.com/journal/index.htm.
- *Billboard*: billboard.com/.
- *Bitch Media*: bitchmedia.org/.
- "Category: Pop Culture," *The Nerve Blog*: sites.bu.edu/ombs/category/pop-culture/.
- *Cultural Politics.net*: culturalpolitics.net/.
- *Department of Popular Culture*: bgsu.edu/arts-and-sciences/cultural-and-critical-studies/popular-culture.html.
- *ESPN*: espn.go.com/.
- *Images: A Journal of Film and Popular Culture*: imagesjournal.com/index.html.
- *Journal of Popular Culture*: journalofpopularculture.com/.

---

savetheinternet.com/sti-home; Katrina VandenHuevel, "Net Neutrality Essential to Our Democracy," *Washington Post* 2 December 2014 at washingtonpost.com/opinions/katrina-vanden-heuvel-net-neutrality-essential-to-our-democracy/2014/12/02/ab85a54e-799e-11e4-84d4-7c896b90abdc_story.html.

- *The Journal of Religion and Popular Culture*: muse.jhu.edu/journals/journal_of_religion_and_popular_culture/.
- "List of Best Pop Culture News Sites and Blogs": infoblizzard.com/ib-resources/list-of-best-pop-culture-news-sites-blogs-on-the-web-2015.
- *People*: people.com/people/.
- "Pop & Culture": fusion.net/section/pop-culture/.
- "Pop Cult," *Info-Blizzard*: infoblizzard.com/pop-cult. html.
- "Pop Culture," *BuzzFeed*: buzzfeed.com/tag/pop_culture.
- "Pop Culture," *CBS-This Morning*: cbsnews.com/cbs-this-morning/pop-culture/.
- "Pop Culture," *Mashable*: mashable.com/category/pop-culture/.
- "Pop Culture," *NBC News*: nbcnews.com/pop-culture.
- "Pop Culture," *Post World War II American Literature and Culture Database*: english.berkeley.edu/Postwar/pop.html.
- "Pop Culture," *Xmarks*: xmarks.com/topic/pop_culture.
- *Pop Dose*: popdose.com/.
- *PopMatters*: popmatters.com/.

- *Popular Culture*: sinq-clusters.unst.pdx.edu/cluster/popular-culture.
- "Popular Culture and Philosophy": opencourtbooks.com/categories/pcp.htm.
- *Popular Culture and Philosophy*: philosophynow.org/issues/64.
- *Popular Culture Studies*: popularculturestudies.osu.edu/.
- *Popular Culture Studies*: wku.edu/pop/.
- *RetroWaste*: retrowaste.com/.
- *Rolling Stone*: rollingstone.com/.
- *Sports Illustrated*: si.com/.
- *Star Trek*: startreck.com.
- *TMZ*: tmz.com/.
- *TrekNews*: treknews.net.
- "Top 25 Blogs in Pop Culture," *Blog Rank*: blogmetrics.org/pop_culture.

Topic 3

Diversity in Action: Korean Americans

One of the diverse segments of America is the population of Korean Americans. *The Rise of Asian Americans* from the Pew Research Foundation gives a quick overview of the history and current state of various Asian- American populations.[1)]

According to the Pew Foundation, Korean immigration to the U.S. began in the early 20th century when over 7,000 Koreans came to Hawaii to work on plantations. About 40% of them were Christians, which might help explain the fact that a majority of Korean Americans now identify as Christian.

Not many Koreans immigrated to the U.S. until after 1965 because, for much of the 20th Century, Asian immigration was strictly limited in the U.S. Asian immigrants were ineligible to become American citizens for much of that time. In 1965, the immigration laws were changed to allow more Asians to enter the U.S. and to become naturalized citizens.

The Korean American population was estimated at 1.26 million adults (out of almost 309 million people) in the 2010 census. The Pew Foundation reports that Korean

1) Available here: pewsocialtrends.org/files/2013/04/Asian-Americans-new-full-report-04-2013.pdf from pewsocialtrends.org/asianamericans/.

Americans comprise about 10% of the total of people of Asian heritage in the U.S.

Among the interesting statistics compiled by Pew surveys are these findings:

- 79% of adult Korean Americans in the United States are foreign born, compared with 74% of all adult Asian Americans and 16% of all adults in the U.S.
- 67% of Korean American adults are U.S. citizens, lower than the 70% share among the overall adult Asian American population and the national share of 91%.
- 54% of Korean Americans speak English proficiently, compared with 63% of all Asian Americans and 90% of the U.S. population overall.
- Among Korean Americans ages 25 and older, 53% have obtained at least a bachelor's degree; this is higher than the overall Asian American share of 49% as well as the national share of 28%.
- Median annual personal earnings for Korean American full-time, year-round workers is higher than the median for all U.S. adults.
- Across U.S. Asian American groups, Korean Americans seem to be more strongly connected to their intra-ethnic communities. They are the most likely to say that all or most of their friends share the same ethnic heritage (58%).

- Compared with other U.S. Asian American groups, Korean Americans are among the most likely to say that it is very important to them that future generations of Koreans living in the U.S. speak their ancestral language (62%).
- Korean Americans are more likely than U.S. Asians from other groups to say that parents from their country of origin put too much academic pressure on their children (60%).
- 71% of Korean Americans identify as Christian, 61% as Protestant and 10% as Catholic, compared to 42% for all Asian Americans and 75% for the overall U.S. population. Only 6% of Korean Americans identify as Buddhist. This compares to Korea, where 18% of the people identify as Protestant, 11% as Catholic, 23% as Buddhist, and 53% as without belief.[2] Whichever set of statistics for Korean religion one chooses, the difference between Korea and Korean America is large.

Q : What do you think might be some reasons for the religious differences between Koreans and Korean Americans?

Q : Which of the other statistics are most interesting to you? Why?

2) Donald Baker, *Korean Spirituality* (University of Hawai'i Press, 2008), 4.

To learn more about ordinary individual Korean Americans and the diversity of that ethnic group, browse *I Am Korean American* (iamkoreanamerican.com), an online social network.

Besides the 2012 popularity of Psy's "Gangnam Style," other aspects of Korea and other Asian cultures have been embraced by Americans of diverse ethnic backgrounds. The meetings of East and West often create uniquely Korean American or Asian American cultural artifacts.

One such meeting place is the "kimchi taco truck." The popularity of those trucks reaches from the west coast to the east coast of America. Make an internet search for "kimchi taco truck images" and see what you find.

Chris Cockren writes about the east coast in "Kimchi Taco: Food Truck Paradise" on the *Shared Appetite* website. Cockren writes, "Combining traditional Korean flavors with comfort foods we Americans love, the Kimchi Taco Truck has rapidly become one of my favorite food trucks in all of NYC. The flavors are bold, the ingredients are fresh, the prices are great, the staff is friendly, and most of all, it's so delicious."[3)]

Erich Redson writes about the west coast in "Kogi Korean BBQ Taco Truck, Los Angeles" on the *L.A. Taco* website. Redson writes, "Is there anything more Los Angeles then a Korean BBQ Taco Truck that cruises the streets delivering high quality cuisine to the city's taco

3) sharedappetite.com/eat/kimchi-taco/

lifestyle hubs? We salute the Kogi truck and hope it is the inspiration for many more."[4)]

The New York Times, among other places, frequently has articles about Korea and Korean America – especially about the food. Find some of the online articles on the list below.

- "2014 In Review: Korean Food Had a Ridiculously Big Year in America" by Matt Rodbard at *Foodrepublic.com* 30 December 2014.[5)]
- "How To Eat Korean Barbecue, With Deuki Hong," a video from *Foodrepublic.com* 16 February 2016.[6)]
- "36 Hours in Koreatown, Los Angeles" by Finn-Olaf Jones, *NYTimes.com* 11 February 2015.[7)]
- "At *Insa* in Brooklyn, a Mix of Karaoke and Korean Barbecue" by Alan Feuer, *NYTimes.com* 2 January 2016.[8)]
- "In Queens, Kimchi Is Just the Start: Pete Wells Explores Korean Restaurants in Queens" by Pete Wells, *NYTimes.com* 16 December 2014.[9)]

---

4) lataco.com/kogi-korean-bbq-taco-truck-los-angeles/

5) foodrepublic.com/2014/12/30/2014-review-korean-food-had-ridiculously-big-year

6) foodrepublic.com/2016/02/16/video-how-to-eat-korean-barbecue-with-deuki hong/

7) nytimes.com/2015/02/15/travel/what-to-do-in-koreatown-los-angeles.html

8) nytimes.com/2016/01/03/nyregion/korean-barbecue-and-karaoke-in-brooklyn-at-insa.html

9) nytimes.com/2014/12/17/dining/critics-notebook-pete-wells-explores-

- "At *Kichin* in Brooklyn, Korean Fried Chicken and Mighty Rice Balls" by Ligaya Mishan, *NYTimes.com* 11 February 2016.[10)]
- "Restaurant Review: Seoulite's Owners Rebuild with Authentic Korean Food" by Fran Schumer, *NYTimes.com* 17 September 2015.[11)]
- "Cooking With Kimchi" by David Tanis, *NYTimes.com* 20 January 2015.[12)]
- And here is one that is not about food: "Why a Generation of Adoptees Is Returning to South Korea" by Maggie Jones, *NYTimes.com* 14 January 2015.[13)]
- And here is one from a different source: "13 Korean Food Trucks We Love," *Kimchi Chronicles Blog* 14 February 2012.[14)]

Those articles will give you an idea about how Korean culture, especially Korean food culture, has influenced American life. Food is definitely an important part of popular

---

korean-restaurants-in-queens.html#

10) nytimes.com/2016/02/17/dining/hungry-city-kichin-williamsburg-brooklyn.html

11) nytimes.com/2015/09/20/nyregion/restaurant-review-seoulites-own-ersrebuild-with-authentic-korean-food.html

12) nytimes.com/2015/01/21/dining/cooking-with-kimchi.html

13) nytimes.com/2015/01/18/magazine/why-a-generation-of-adoptees-is-returning-to-south-korea.html

14) kimchichronicles.tv/2012/02/13-korean-food-trucks-we-love/. Notice that this one is about "love" and is published on Valentine's Day.

culture. Like other aspects of American culture, the export of American food culture has influenced Korean eating habits. Think about the popularity of fast food in Korea, for instance.

With that American influence in mind, consider this:

Q : What American food influences Korean eating habits the most?

People might answer that question in different ways. Some say hamburgers; some say pizza; some say other things. Many Koreans are surprised by the answer I would give: hot peppers, 고추 (*gochu*). That's right, peppers come from America, although not recently, and not from the U.S. In the 16th century, Portuguese traders brought peppers from Central America to Japan, and from Japan, peppers made their way to Korea. Before that, all kimchi was white kimchi.[15)]

You might explore Asian American presence in popular culture other than food, as well. To hear two Korean American spoken-word artists, search an online video source for Franny Choi and Ed Bok Lee, or check out their websites at *frannychoi.com* and *edboklee.com*. The Asian-American spoken-word community in the U.S. includes a lot more

15) To read about that fact and many other interesting things about the connection between Asian and American food cultures, you might look at Robert Ji-song Ku's book *Dubious Gastronomy: The Cultural Politics of Eating Asian in the U.S.A.* (University of Hawaii Press, 2014). The information about peppers coming to Korea is on page 91.

people than those two, however. For instance, here are three videos about the Hmong hip-hop community in Minnesota:

- "Hmong Hip Hop Heritage"[16]
- "Closing Performance by Tou SaiKo Lee"[17]
- "State of the Re: Union—Twin Cities: Hmong Hip-Hop"[18]

As you will see from the spoken-word videos, the mixing of cultures in Asia America is not always easy. For an example of tension between Korean tradition and the American experience, see Margaret Cho's story about an American cultural difference of opinion about tattoos.

Cho is a well-known Korean American comedian. The story, which is on the *Jezebel* website, is titled "In a Room Full of Naked Koreans, Margaret Cho's Body Is an Unwelcome Sight."[19] It is a story about how she was asked to put on clothes in a Los Angeles *jimjilbang* (public bath house) because the older Korean immigrant women did not want to see her tattoos.

We might think of Cho's body tattoos, which are displayed in a photograph that accompanies the article, as a representation of American individualism. That

---

16) *NYTimes Magazine* 8 May 2008. nytimes.com/video/magazine/1194817116411/hmong-hip-hop-heritage.html

17) youtube.com/watch?v=AHdwMUCTq74

18) youtube.com/watch?v=oSDDN3wV7tY

19) jezebel.com/5992256/in-a-room-full-of-naked-koreans-margaret-chos-body-is-an-unwelcome-sight

individualism is often seen as an essential American trait (see Chapter 5). The older Korean American women who insisted she wear clothes might represent the migration of Korean collective culture to the U.S. Maybe we can call that *uri*-ness (우리-ness; we-ness) rather than individuality. Perhaps that collective perspective is now a part of American diversity.

Recently Korean television dramas have become popular in the U.S. These websites and online essays indicate that those dramas have found a niche in American popular culture:

- *Drama Fever* (www.dramafever.com)
- *Drama Beans* (www.dramabeans.com)
- *All Korean Drama* (allkoreandrama.com)
- *All about Korean Drama* (www.koreandrama.org)
- *Viki* (www.viki.com)
- "Read Princeton Professor Uwe Reinhardt's Lecture on Korean Drama" by CoCo Kdrama on *Drama Fever* 11 February 2014.[20)]
- "Korean TV Dramas Surprisingly Embraced by U.S. Audiences" from 8 August 2006. According to this essay, more than 90% of K-drama fans in the U.S. are not of Korean heritage.[21)]

---

20) www.dramafever.com/news/read-princeton-professor-uwe-reinhardts-lecture-on-korean-drama

21) www.prnewswire.com/news-releases/korean-tv-dramas-surprisingly-embraced-by-us-audiences-56045202.html

- "Korean Drama Fever Hits U.S." *Inquirer.net* 18 September 2014.[22)]

For other Asian American literary arts, see *The Asian American Writers Workshop* website (aaww.org, opencitymag.com). Located in New York City, *AAWW* shows how Korean Americans, as well as other Asian Americans, influence the literature and society of the U.S. Another organization in New York is *The MinKwon Center for Community Action* (minkwon.org) in Flushing. This is an Asian-American community advocacy organization. That area of New York also chose Ronald Kim as the first-ever Korean American elected to the New York State Assembly in 2012.

FOR FURTHER CONSIDERATION

Choose one of the articles on Korean America from the *NY Times* and other sources. What did you learn from the article? What are some of the most interesting parts of the article? Did it have a positive or negative depiction of Korea or Korean America? What comments on or criticisms of the article might you have? How does Korean America as described in the article compare to Korea itself?

Compare the websites about Korean drama (*Drama Fever, Drama Beans, All Korean Drama, All about Korean*

22) entertainment.inquirer.net/152866/korean-drama-fever-hits-us

Drama, Viki) for what they offer to viewers. Which are most informative? Which are easiest to use? How could they be improved?

Comment on one or more of the articles about Korean dramas in the U.S. What did you learn from the article(s)? What are some of the most interesting parts of the article(s)? Did it/they give a positive or negative depiction of Korean Drama and its American fans? What other comments on or criticisms of the article might you have?

Topic 4

The Idea of America

The fight against racial discrimination mentioned in Chapter 1 has been one means of getting closer to the idea expressed in the founding document of America, the *Declaration of Independence*. Tradition says the *Declaration* was signed on July 4, 1776 in Philadelphia, Pennsylvania. Before this *Declaration*, there was no nation that we today think of as "America." The U.S. was still part of England. In 1776, no one was sure that there would be such a country as the U.S.A. No one could be sure until after the American Revolutionary War, when the British army surrendered in 1781 and England recognized the new nation in 1783.

> The key ideas of the *Declaration of Independence* occur near the beginning:
>
> We hold these truths to be self-evident, that all men are created equal, that they are endowed by their Creator with certain unalienable Rights, that among these are Life, Liberty and the pursuit of Happiness. That to secure these rights, Governments are instituted among Men, deriving their just powers from the consent of the governed.[1)]

1) The entire document is available at "America's Founding Documents,"

As the *Declaration of Independence* and its historical importance indicate, America is not just a physical or geographic place. It is also an imagined place, an idea of a nation. Indeed, Benedict Anderson has famously argued that all modern nations are "imagined communities."[2)]

Q : What do you think are some of the most important ideas in the passage from the *Declaration of Independence* quoted above?

If we look more closely at the first sentence of the excerpt from the *Declaration of Independence*, we can begin to see how the American community has been imagined. First, those early U.S. Americans believed in some things that were true, and that they were obviously true, or "self-evident." These true things needed no argument and could be assumed. "These truths" are the assumptions on which the nation is founded.

There are two major assumptions:

- all men are created equal
- they are endowed by their Creator with certain unalienable Rights

---

National Archives : archives.gov/exhibits/charters/declaration.html.

2) *Imagined Communities: Reflections on the Origin and Spread of Nationalism* (NY: Verso, 1983 & 2016).

The first assumption is about human equality. In the 18th century, the phrase "all *men*" referred to "all *people*," all human beings, not just adult males. In reality, of course, most of those "founding fathers," the representatives who signed the *Declaration of Independence*, did not *really* believe that all human beings were created equally. Maybe some of them actually believed that only all white males with property deserved equality. All of them were property-owning white men.

Along with that equality came certain rights, which is the second "self-evident" assumption. Those rights—human rights—were "unalienable," which means they cannot be taken away, that they naturally belong to everyone. Those rights are "Life, Liberty and the pursuit of Happiness." These are nice ideas.

The reality, however, was different. Women were not really considered equal to men. Non-white people were not really considered equal to white people. When the *Declaration of Independence* was written, black slavery was still legal in much of America. The history of voting rights in the U.S. shows that lack of equality. Non-white people were not given the right to vote until 1870, when the 15th *amendment* (an amendment is a change) to the U.S. Constitution was *ratified* (approved by voters in two-thirds of the states). That amendment guaranteed that all men could vote, no matter their "race, color, or previous condition of servitude." Women of any race or color were not guaranteed the right to vote until the 19th amendment was ratified in 1920. Even after those guarantees, however, some states, particularly southern states, found ways to keep black people from voting until the Civil Rights laws of the 1960s were passed. Again today, some southern states are attempting to circumvent those laws and restrict voting rights for black people.

Those examples show that *ideals* of the U.S. are not always demonstrated in reality. The *ideal* of universal human equality sounds very good, but the U.S. has perhaps never fully lived up to its ideals. I think most people will agree that everyone should have the rights to "Life, Liberty, and the pursuit of Happiness." We might agree with the words, but, sometimes, we might hinder some groups or individuals from that pursuit. Furthermore, we might not all agree on exactly what the "pursuit of Happiness" means.

FOR FURTHER CONSIDERATION

Here is "the three-fifths compromise" to the U.S. Constitution, ratified in 1787. It is located in Article 1, Section 2, Paragraph 3:

> Representatives and direct Taxes shall be apportioned among the several States which may be included within this Union, according to their respective Numbers, which shall be determined by adding to the whole Number of free Persons, including those bound to Service for a Term of Years, and excluding Indians not taxed, three fifths of all other Persons.

Who are "all other Persons" (those people who are not "free Persons" and are not "Indians")? How much of a "free Person" is counted for taxation and representation? How much of an "other Person" is counted for taxation and representation? How does this "compromise" contradict the idea that "all men are created equal"?

Topic 5

American Ideas

In their book *American Ways*, which is often used in Korean classes on American society, Maryanne Kearny Datesman, JoAnn Crandall, and Edward N. Kearny identify six fundamental American beliefs and values, placing them all in the context of "racial, ethnic, religious, and cultural diversity." Those six values are:[1)]

- **Individual Freedom**: including *political* freedom (democracy); also *personal* freedom – I can say and do what I want, as long as I don't hurt anyone else; there are possible problems in conflating *individualism* and *freedom*; see if you can identify this value in the beginning of the U.S. Declaration of Independence.
- **Self Reliance**: a possible consequence of individual freedom; financial and emotional independence from parents, often at 18 or 21;"Americans believe they should take care of themselves, solve their own problems, 'stand on their own two feet.'"
- **Equality of Opportunity**: America has no social classes (no aristocracy) – America has *social* mobility;

1) *American Ways*, 3rd edition (Longman, 2005), 25-33.

each individual should have an equal opportunity to succeed; this involves the concept of "fair play"; the U.S. is a supposedly *egalitarian* society.

- **Competition**: a possible consequence of equal opportunity; life is a race for success (often *economic* success); everyone has an equal opportunity to fail as well as to succeed; America is a society of *winners* and *losers*; the American sense of competition is often developed by competitive sports.
- **Material Wealth**: there is an emphasis on *economic* mobility, as in the many "rags to riches" stories; this is a major component of the "American Dream"; *materialism* might suggest greed, however, which is not a good thing, as most people would agree; wealth is a widely (not unanimously) accepted measure of social status.
- **Hard Work**: this is necessary for material wealth (an idea that ignores those who are born into wealthy families); even if I do not achieve all my dreams, my children will be able to achieve theirs; if I work hard, I *will* succeed and achieve the American Dream.

Remember, not every American believes or values all of these things, but these six values and beliefs are recognized by most Americans as ideas that contribute to the *myth* of America. Some people might add other things. Many people would add "Christianity" to the list. Others might add "innovation" or "creativity." Still others might add *mobility*—geographical mobility, social mobility, economic mobility. The love of cars is part of Americans' mobility, the frequent desire to go new places and see new things, to escape from the confines of everyday life. As an example of how all these values may not be shared by all Americans, I might take "material wealth" off of my own personal list of values, although I would probably agree that, in general, the desire for wealth is an American trait. I have met or read about many wealthy people whom I do not regard highly. Perhaps taking material wealth off the list reflects another value: individual freedom. Often we equate wealth with success, and we admire success.

Q : When people say, "He is a very successful man," they usually mean he has made a lot of money. How else can we define success?

Most of those beliefs and values are basically positive characteristics, although they may have some negative aspects. Some people could identify more clearly negative American traits.

Q : See if you can guess what goes in each blank space of the following joke. What negative American characteristic is implied?

What do you call a person who can speak two languages? ______

What do you call a person who can speak several languages? ______

What do you call a person who can speak just one language? ______[2]

For another way to think about material wealth, consider the following analogy from sports: "He was born on third base and thinks he hit a triple."

Q : What do you think that analogy means? Does it apply to people who were born into rich families or poor families? How would you explain your answer?

In thinking about the *belief* that hard work pays off in America because there is equality of opportunity, we might consider that studies have shown that people from many other countries have a better chance of moving up in class than do Americans. Jason DeParle, for instance, makes the following observations in an article for the January 1, 2012 *NY Times*:

Benjamin Franklin did it. Henry Ford did it. And

2) The answers: bilingual; polylingual or multilingual; American.

> American life is built on the faith that others can do it, too: *rise from humble origins to economic heights.* "Movin' on up," George Jefferson-style[3] is not only a sitcom song but a civil religion. But many researchers have reached a conclusion that turns conventional wisdom on its head: *Americans enjoy less economic mobility than their peers in Canada and much of Western Europe.* . . . In 2006 Professor Corak reviewed more than 50 studies of nine countries. He ranked Canada, Norway, Finland and Denmark as the most mobile, with the United States and Britain roughly tied at the other extreme. Sweden, Germany, and France were scattered across the middle. (emphasis added)

Being a common *belief* does not make something *true.*

FOR FURTHER CONSIDERATION

American Values Expressed in Popular Culture. Identify various American beliefs and values as expressed in the following. The web addresses may have changed, but this television commercial and these songs should be available online. I have given you some notes for "Wide Open Spaces" and "Hey, Good Lookin." Work on the others yourselves.

3) George Jefferson was a central character in *The Jeffersons* an American TV situation-comedy, or 'sitcom' (CBS, 1975-85); the Jeffersons are a black couple who rose from poverty to affluence.

- "American As" Jack Daniels commercial.[4]
- "Hey, Good Lookin'," a country song by Hank Williams.[5]
- "Wide Open Spaces," another country song, this one by the Dixie Chicks.[6]
- "Wandering Star," from the movie *Paint Your Wagons*.[7]
- "Oh Freedom," an old song created by American slaves, a "spiritual."[8]

Listen to the Jack Daniels commercial and write down as much as you can hear, then listen to the songs. As you listen to the songs, think about American characteristics we have mentioned, but also others we may not have mentioned. You can find the lyrics to the songs online. Some good sources for lyrics are *azlyrics.com, metrolyrics.com*, and *genius.com.*

4) www.youtube.com/watch?v=AXBzgAWv1TE

5) www.youtube.com/watch?v=95aP0OWx4jY

6) www.youtube.com/watch?v=bmBW3yRxKUY

7) www.youtube.com/watch?v=pE9vc2cO170

8) Two versions: www.youtube.com/watch?v=cbTgsP9Rs0s&feature=related, with Renée Fleming, Joan Baez, Suzanne Vega, and Lou Reed; www.youtube.com/watch?v=yHmUPqI6w9g

Hey, Good Lookin' (1951)

Some notes and questions.

- "What's cooking?" is an old-fashioned greeting that means "What are you doing?" or "What are your plans?" When he asks if they can find a new "recipe," he is building on the metaphor of "cooking." A "recipe" gives the ingredients and directions for making a particular kind of food. To what kind of "food" does this song refer, do you think?
- What is "soda pop"? They are soft drinks (음료) like Coke or Pepsi or Fanta.
- A "date book" is a little notebook in which a young man would write down the names and phone numbers of young women he wants to ask for a date. This "date" is not a month and day but a meeting for a young couple to enjoy themselves.

Wide Open Spaces (1998)

Some notes and questions.

- In this song, to "strike out" means to leave one place, often permanently, and go somewhere else. (In baseball, it means something different.)
- To have a place in the clouds means to have dreams, things that have not yet become real. We often say of a dreamer, someone who may not be very practical,

"He has his head in the clouds."

- On the other hand, to have a foundation of stone means to be practical, to have a strong base in the world—a foundation is the base of a building. Carpenters first make a foundation, then build the building on top of it. Good parents give their children a strong "foundation" for success in the world. One source for the metaphor comes from a passage in the Bible.

    Jesus said, "Therefore everyone who hears these words of mine and puts them into practice is like a wise man who built his house on the rock. The rain came down, the streams rose, and the winds blew and beat against that house; yet it did not fall, because it had its foundation on the rock. But everyone who hears these words of mine and does not put them into practice is like a foolish man who built his house on sand. The rain came down, the streams rose, and the winds blew and beat against that house, and it fell with a great crash" (Matthew 7: 24-27, New International Version).

- After we get lessons in school, how does the teacher know whether or not we have learned the material? He or she gives a *test*. We can apply that idea to life as well.
- Who doesn't know? Nobody doesn't know; everybody

knows – this is a common experience; this young woman is not special. This is just like the Korean rhetorical question, "누구 몰라요?"

- Americans are independent – she is going off on her own, without help from others. Also, she knows how to take care of her car. We know this because her dad reminds her to check the oil – that is the engine oil that keeps the car running smoothly. She does not need to take her car to an auto mechanic because she can do it herself.
- Americans are dreamers – a place in the clouds.
- Americans are practical – foundation of stone. Her head might be in the clouds but her feet are on the ground, which suggests a realistic, practical person. Thus, having big dreams is realistic in America, according to this song.
- Americans are mobile – in this case, the person is going out west, leaving her hometown for some other place. That is a very American story – after all, most Americans are descendants of people who left home for some other place. This tradition of leaving is demonstrated by the mother in the song, who remembers when she herself set out on her own. This belief in mobility is not just geographic; it is also social and economic. Americans are not fixed by a class system, and economic success or improvement is possible for everyone (at least that

is what many Americans believe).

- Americans are adventuresome—she doesn't know what the future holds, she hasn't yet guessed, but she is excited to find out.
- Americans are willing to fail, and they learn by failure—she is willing to make "her big mistakes."
- Women are equal to men in capability—while taking care of the car may be considered by some to be a man's job, this young woman can take care of her own car. Her mother also remembers leaving home when she was young.

Topic 6

American Exceptionalism, Manifest Destiny

AMERICAN EXCEPTIONALISM

In March, 2008, before Barack Obama became the 44th president of the United States, he gave a speech on race in America in which he recognized that America's past was not perfect for black people. He said, "I am married to a black American who carries within her the blood of slaves and slave owners — an inheritance we pass on to our two precious daughters." In that speech, he insisted that America is a unique country in the world, saying, "I will never forget that in no other country on Earth is my story even possible." In that claim of American uniqueness, he echoes a common American belief: the belief in *American exceptionalism.* According to that belief, America is like no other country that has ever existed in the world. It is a special country, and it is superior in that specialness. This idea is a foundation of American culture for many in the U.S., and even for some people from other countries.

According to Trevor B. McCrisken in the *Encyclopedia of the New American Nation,*[1] "Alexis de Tocqueville was

1) "Exceptionalism": americanforeignrelations.com/E-N/Exceptionalism.html; also "Exceptionalism — The Belief in American Exceptionalism": americanforeignrelations.com/E-N/Exceptionalism-The-belief-in-american-

the first to use the term 'exceptional' to describe the United States and the American people in his classic work *Democracy in America* (1835 - 1840)." While it may not have been de Tocqueville's exact intention, that term has taken on the meaning that "the United States is an extraordinary nation with a special role to play in human history; a nation that is not only unique but also superior." America is considered to be a special nation because of the professed belief that "all men are created equal." American democracy is seen as a beacon of hope for all of the world.

Of course, not every American embraces exceptionalism. As McCrisken notes,

> Certainly not all Americans believe whole-heartedly in all these aspects of American exceptionalism. Many Americans are all too aware that major problems exist within their society, many of which they may never adequately solve. They accept that in an increasingly interdependent world the United States cannot claim dominion in international affairs and that when they do intervene abroad, Americans very often undermine the very principles they claim to be defending.

One of the earliest expressions of an idea that has been used to bolster beliefs in exceptionalism comes from John Winthrop's sermon, "A Model of Christian Charity." Winthrop preached this sermon in 1630. He and his fellow

---

exceptionalism.html

Puritans sailed from England to America to establish what would become the city of Boston. Winthrop told his fellow migrants, "For we must consider that we shall be as a city upon a hill. The eyes of all people are upon us." He takes the idea of the city on the hill from a speech by Jesus recorded in the Bible, the fifth chapter of the *Gospel According to Matthew*. Just before Jesus mentions the city on the hill, he says to his listeners, "You are the light of the world." When he mentions the city, he says that a city built on a hill cannot be hidden. The light that shines from that city in Winthrop's sermon is the light of American exceptionalism to many in the U.S. For them, American democracy and freedom, as expressed in the *Declaration of Independence*, are that light of the world.

MANIFEST DESTINY

The concept of "manifest destiny" is a particular aspect of missionary exceptionalism. The idea was first put into print by John L. O'Sullivan in an essay titled "Annexation" published in *United States Magazine and Democratic Review* in 1845.[2] He argued that the U.S. should *annex* Oregon and Mexican territories. This was a time of great westward expansion for the U.S., which more than tripled in size from 1803 to 1853.

2) Text available from Pedro Domínguez Caballero de Rodas, "Victorianism, Manifest Destiny," *Textos Históricos y Culturales Anglonorteamericanos*: pdcrodas.webs.ull.es/anglo/OSullivanAnnexation.pdf

O'Sullivan claimed it was "our [the U.S.'s] manifest destiny to overspread the continent allotted by Providence." He insisted it was "the manifest design of Providence in regard to the occupation of this continent." He felt that the U.S. takeover of more land "was not only inevitable, but the most natural, right and proper thing in the world." In discussing California, which at that time was a Mexican possession, he made clear that white people whose ancestors came from Northern Europe were the chosen people. He wrote that "the Anglo-Saxon foot is already on [California's] borders. Already the advance guard of the irresistible army of Anglo-Saxon emigration has begun to pour down upon it, armed with the plough and the rifle, and marking its trail with schools and colleges, courts and representative hails, mills and meeting-houses."

To be "manifest" means to be made obvious, to be revealed by God in clear and obvious ways; "destiny," of course, means the future predetermined for a person, group of people, or, in this case, a nation. When O'Sullivan uses the word "Providence" with the upper-case, he uses it as an alternative term for God. Thus, manifest destiny is the destiny planned by God for white people to take over all of North America. That emphasis on the U.S. as a nation especially chosen and favored by God has recurred throughout American history.

For instance, most of America's 50 states require that students recite the "Pledge of Allegiance" or perform some other patriotic duty at the beginning of each school day.

The Pledge contains the statement that the U.S. is "one nation, under God." Here is the entire Pledge: "I pledge allegiance to the flag of the United States of America, and to the republic for which it stands, one nation under God, indivisible, with liberty and justice for all." The Pledge was originally written in 1892, but the words "under God" were not added until 1954, when America was frightened by the rise of communism in the world. Communism was against established religions, so adding the words "under God" was a way of expressing anti-communist belief. This was also the time when "In God We Trust" was required by law to be printed on American money: that law was passed in 1956.

Donald M. Scott writes the following in an article titled "The Religious Origins of Manifest Destiny":

> "Manifest Destiny" became first and foremost a call and justification for an American form of imperialism, and neatly summarized the goals of the Mexican War. It claimed that America had a destiny, manifest, i.e., self-evident, from God to occupy the North American continent . . . "Manifest Destiny" was also clearly a racial doctrine of white supremacy . . .
>
> But Manifest Destiny was not simply a cloak for American imperialism and a justification for America's territorial ambitions. It also was firmly anchored in a long standing and deep sense of a special and unique American Destiny, the belief that in the words of

> historian Conrad Cherry, "America is a nation called to a special destiny by God." The notion that there was some providential purpose to the European discovery and eventual conquest of the land masses "discovered" by Christopher Columbus was present from the beginning. Both the Spanish and the French monarchs authorized and financed exploration of the "New World" because, among other things, they considered it their divinely appointed mission to spread Christianity to the New World by converting the natives to Christianity. Coming later to the venture, the British and especially the New England Puritans carried with them a demanding sense of Providential purpose.[3)]

A contemporary echo of this 19-century concept appears in a report about George W. Bush's reaction to the destruction of the World Trade Towers on September 11, 2001. That reaction led to ongoing conflicts in Iraq and Afghanistan. According to the report, "Bush believes he was called by God to lead the nation at this time."[4)] The idea of an American doing the work of God in bringing American influence to another part of the world seems a lot like manifest destiny.

Popular culture has reacted to American exceptionalism

---

3) "Teacher Serve," *National Humanities Center*: nationalhumanitiescenter.org/tserve/nineteen/nkeyinfo/mandestiny.htm.

4) Judy Keen, "Strain of Iraq War Showing on Bush, Those Who Know Him Say," *USA Today* 2 April 2003. usatoday.com/news/washington/2003-04-01-bush-cover_x.htm.

and its purported manifest destiny in various ways. For instance, in 2003, just before George W. Bush invaded Iraq, one of the Dixie Chicks (the country group that sang "Wide Open Spaces") said that she was ashamed that Bush was from Texas because she thought that invading Iraq was wrong. Many country-music fans are very patriotic, even nationalistic, and the Dixie Chicks' music was not played on country-music stations for several years after that comment.[5)]

FOR FURTHER CONSIDERATION

Many people continue to believe in the idea of American and in America's exceptionalism. Barack Obama has reflected that belief in many of his public statements, as in the following two excerpts from different speeches. The President before him, George W. Bush, likewise expressed such beliefs. Compare and contrast the three excerpts below. What similar ideas do you find in each excerpt? What are some of the differences? Which excerpt emphasizes ideas that resemble "manifest destiny"? Be sure to give examples in your answers.

The first excerpt is from Obama's speech on race in America that he gave on March 18, 2008:[6)]

---

5) Greg Mitchell, "Ten Years Ago Today a Dixie Chick Dared to Hit Bush on War—and a Hate Campaign Began." *The Nation* 19 March 2013. thenation.com/article/ten-years-ago-today-dixie-chick-dared-hit-bush-war-and-hate-campaign-began/

6) For the entire speech, go to huffingtonpost.com/2008/03/18/obama-race-speech-read-th_n_92077.html

> I am the son of a black man from Kenya and a white woman from Kansas. I was raised with the help of a white grandfather who survived a Depression to serve in Patton's Army during World War II and a white grandmother who worked on a bomber assembly line at Fort Leavenworth while he was overseas. I've gone to some of the best schools in America and lived in one of the world's poorest nations. I am married to a black American who carries within her the blood of slaves and slave owners — an inheritance we pass on to our two precious daughters. I have brothers, sisters, nieces, nephews, uncles and cousins, of every race and every hue, scattered across three continents, and for as long as I live, I will never forget that in no other country on Earth is my story even possible.
>
> It's a story that hasn't made me the most conventional candidate. But it is a story that has seared into my genetic makeup the idea that this nation is more than the sum of its parts — that out of many, we are truly one.

The second excerpt is from Obama's acceptance speech on election night, 2008:[7]

> If there is anyone out there who still doubts that America is a place where all things are possible, who

7) For the entire speech, go to elections.nytimes.com/2008/results/president/speeches/obama-victory-speech#

> still wonders if the dream of our founders is alive in our time, who still questions the power of our democracy, tonight is your answer.
>
> To those — to those who would tear the world down: We will defeat you. To those who seek peace and security: We support you. And to all those who have wondered if America's beacon still burns as bright: Tonight we proved once more that the true strength of our nation comes not from the might of our arms or the scale of our wealth, but from the enduring power of our ideals: democracy, liberty, opportunity and unyielding hope.
>
> That's the true genius of America: that America can change. Our union can be perfected. What we've already achieved gives us hope for what we can and must achieve tomorrow.

The third excerpt is from "The National Security Strategy of the United States of America," signed by George W. Bush on September 17, 2002. The preface to that document ties personal freedom to free enterprise: [8)]

> The great struggles of the twentieth century between liberty and totalitarianism ended with . . . a single sustainable model for national success: freedom, democracy, and free enterprise. . . . People everywhere

8) For the entire document, go to state.gov/documents/organization/63562.pdf.

want to be able to speak freely; choose who will govern them; worship as they please; educate their children—male and female; own property; and enjoy the benefits of their labor. These values of freedom are right and true for every person, in every society—and the duty of protecting these values against their enemies is the common calling of freedom-loving people across the globe and across the ages.

Today, the United States enjoys a position of unparalleled military strength and great economic and political influence. In keeping with our heritage and principles, we do not use our strength to press for unilateral advantage. We seek instead to create a balance of power that favors human freedom: conditions in which all nations and all societies can choose for themselves the rewards and challenges of political and economic liberty. . . .

The United States will use this moment of opportunity to extend the benefits of freedom across the globe. We will actively work to bring the hope of democracy, development, free markets, and free trade to every corner of the world. . . . Free trade and free markets have proven their ability to lift whole societies out of poverty—so the United States will work with individual nations, entire regions, and the entire global trading community to build a world that trades in freedom and therefore grows in prosperity.

At the time of an earlier war (Vietnam), a young singer addressed the idea of manifest destiny in a song titled "With God on Our Side." That singer was Bob Dylan, who became one of America's most well-known popular singers and was awarded the Nobel Prize in Literature for 2016. "With God on Our Side" came out in 1964. Bob Dylan opposed the idea of manifest destiny. His song shows how popular music can function as *counter* culture, presenting ideas that oppose the mainstream. Find the lyrics and a video of the song on the internet.[9] Look at how he uses *irony* to question the idea that God is on "our" (the U.S.'s) side, which is, in a nutshell, the idea of manifest destiny. Be able to identify how we can know that the singer does not really believe that God is on America's side.

9) youtube.com/watch?v=cAgAvnvXF9U; youtube.com/watch?v=BfHLYIms97A; youtube.com/watch?v=M7FKyouUIsQ.

Topic 7

Sports in America－I

Sports are very popular in America. Almost every year, the Super Bowl is the most watched television program in the U.S. The Super Bowl is the championship game of the National Football League (NFL), the major professional league of American-style football. Politicians often use sports as a way to bring attention to themselves. For instance, the President of the United States often throws out the first pitch of the World Series, which is the championship series for Major League Baseball (MLB), the major American professional baseball organization, because baseball is "America's game." Sports can become political, as in an online video that brings a little political humor to the topic of baseball. The video is titled "Man vs Child or Bush vs Obama First Ceremonial Pitch." It compares former President George W. Bush (a Republican, the major conservative political party in the U.S.) and former President Barack Obama (a Democrat, the major liberal political party in the U.S.) throwing out a first pitch at a baseball game.[1)]

Why do you think that video might be embarrassing for Democrats? On the other hand, the video titled "Barack Obama drains 3-point jumper on first try in Kuwait" might

1) youtube.com/watch?v=WwXh9J8WLqI

recover a little sporting pride for the Democrats.[2)]

Speaking of politics and sports, read the following, which was taken from the U.S. Embassy. As you read, think about the American beliefs and values reflected in this explanation of sports in the U.S.

Q : Be able to identify those various beliefs and values, and answer these two questions:

What good things about sports are mentioned?

What bad things about sports are mentioned?

From the U.S. Embassy:[3)]

> The important impact of sports on American society is acknowledged by the U.S. Government. The fact that sports and participating in sport activities help individuals develop character, discipline, confidence, self-esteem, and a sense of well-being is especially recognized by The President's Council on Physical Fitness and Sports (PCPFS). It serves as a catalyst to promote, encourage and motivate the development of physical fitness and sports participation for all Amcricans of all ages. The PCPFS believes that physical activity and fitness offers important health benefits. In June

2) youtube.com/watch?v=j87k1j4CpOw

3) "Sports in U.S. Society," *Info-pedia USA*. infopedia.usembassy.or.kr/ENG/_f_1402.html

2002, President Bush presented his Fitness Agenda tasking the council with the communication of his Administration's message on fitness and health.

Sport plays a major role in American society as it accounts for the most popular form of recreation. Many Americans are involved in sports—either as a participant or as a spectator. Amateur sports distinguishes between recreational and competitive sports. Favorite recreational activities include hiking, walking, boating, hunting, and fishing. All of these are liked for the recreational value as well as for exercise. But there are also many other sports activities in America which attract millions of participants for personal enjoyment, the love of competition, and for the benefits of fitness and health. In addition, sport teaches social values like teamwork, sportsmanship, self-discipline, and persistence that are highly regarded in U.S. society.

All these requirements are well covered in team sports such as baseball, basketball, football, volleyball that gained increased emphasis in the 20th century. Individual sports like swimming, golf, tennis, bowling, skiing, and track and field are equally popular.

Americans also take part in sports as spectators—actually at the contest or via television. It is great entertainment for sports fans to watch their teams and athletes competing in professional sports. Favorites are typical American sports like baseball, basketball, and football. In the western states rodeos are also very popular sports events.

Q : In which sports or recreational activities have you participated? Which sports do you like to watch?

Here are the most popular professional team sports in the U.S., depending on how one measures popularity.

- Professional Football (NFL): nfl.com
- Professional Basketball (NBA): nba.com
- Professional Baseball (MLB): mlb.com
- Professional Hockey (NHL): nhl.com
- Professional Soccer (MLS): mlssoccer.com

NASCAR, however, may be the most popular spectator sport in the U.S. NASCAR is the acronym for the National Association for Stock Car Automobile Racing. While other kinds of automobile racing, such as Le Mans road racing, may have originated elsewhere, stock-car racing originated in the U.S.

Determining which sport is most popular in America depends on how that popularity is measured. One way to measure popularity is by how many people actually attend the events. According to the *Forbes* website, in 2012, the last year that NASCAR released statistics, more people attend NASCAR races than attended any other professional sport in the U.S.[4] Football is second for attendance by live spectators.

Another way to measure popularity is by number of television viewers. By that measure, the NFL is the most popular and NASCAR is second.

Yet another way of measuring popularity is by asking people, by taking a survey. In the Harris Poll of most popular sports, which began in 1985 and has been conducted annually since 2002, auto racing (not NASCAR specifically) has never finished higher than fourth. In the 2015 poll, the NFL was first with 33%, followed by MLB (15%), college football (10%), auto racing (6%), NBA (5%), and NHL (5%).[5)]

Of the six professional sports listed above (NFL, NBA, MLB, NHL, MLS, NASCAR), five originated in North America. Only soccer, which most of the rest of the English-speaking world calls football (축구/*chukgu*), originated elsewhere, in England. Of the five sports that originated in North America, one comes from Canada rather than the U.S. That sport is ice hockey. American football, basketball, baseball, and stock-car racing originated in the U.S.

The origins of stock-car racing are quite colorful, and they have an historical connection to the time period of the novel and the film titled *The Great Gatsby*, which will be discussed later. In January, 1920, the 18th Amendment to the U.S. Constitution took effect. That Amendment prohibited the making, transporting, and selling of alcohol.

---

4) Steve Odland, "NASCAR's Back!" 27 February 2012. forbes.com/sites/steveodland/2012/02/27/nascars-back/#451e1ec71c1d

5) theharrispoll.com/sports/Americas_Fav_Sport_2016.html

This Amendment is called "Prohibition." Of course, Prohibition did not mean that people stopped making, transporting, or selling alcohol. Those things were just done secretly and illegally. There could be no legal businesses that sold alcohol, so the "speakeasy" was created. The speakeasy was an illegal or "underground" bar (술집/*suljip*). The *Great Gatsby* has a scene in a speakeasy.

The alcohol that was made illegally was referred to as "moonshine." In order to move moonshine from places where it was made illegally to the speakeasies where it was sold illegally, it had to be transported illegally. Those people who transported moonshine illegally were called "bootleggers." Bootleggers who drove cars often worked on the cars to make them go as fast as possible in the hopes of escaping from police and other government agents.

Those bootleggers with fast cars would sometimes get together and race against one another. When Prohibition ended with the 21st Amendment in 1933, those fast-car driving bootleggers had to find another way to make money, so they took their fast cars and began racing against one another rather than running from the police. Those races needed an organization with an established set of rules. The organization of these races eventually developed into the National Association for Stock Car Automobile Racing—NASCAR.

Although it may no longer be America's most popular

sport, baseball has traditionally been considered "America's pastime" or "America's national pastime." It seems to harken back to a simpler time when the world moved more slowly. Baseball has been mythologized in novels and movies like *The Natural, Bull Durham, Field of Dreams,* and *A League of Their Own*. You could look them up on the internet, and perhaps search for other baseball movies – there are many.

There are many ways to think about sports (or "athletics"). One way is to divide them into team sports and individual sports. Another division is competitive sports and recreational sports or activities. Another is spectator sports and participatory sports.

While baseball may be known as America's national pastime, football is certainly America's most popular team sport, at least as a spectator sport. As noted above, the championship game of the NFL is called the Super Bowl, and it is played in February.

Q : What is a bowl? What is the shape of a large sports stadium? Do you see why football has bowl games?

The Super Bowl is usually the most watched program on television in the U.S. every year. Not everyone watches for the game itself, however. Usually, the half-time show gets more viewers than the game itself. The halftime entertainment is always provided by a major singing star. In 2016, Beyoncé was the big star, and she caused a big controversy when she sang "Formation," a song that addresses racial issues and African-American culture in the U.S.

Another reason people watch the game is for the commercials, which are evaluated for their creativity and humor. Many websites gather online commentary as the game proceeds. A professor from the Communication Department at the college where I taught in the U.S. invited me to a Super Bowl party with his students every year. I declined the invitation because, being a sports fan, I wanted to watch the game, and they watched only the commercials and discussed what made them good or bad from an advertising perspective. If you would like to see some of the commercials, make an internet search for "Best Super Bowl Commercials 2016" (or 2015, 2014, 2013, etc.).

FOR FURTHER CONSIDERATION

As many of the students know, professional baseball us also a popular spectator sport in Korea. A Korean professional baseball game has cheerleaders, group cheers, and songs for each player and situation in a game, but an American professional game has none of those things.

However, American baseball does have one song

that is sung at almost every game. It is sung during the "seventh-inning stretch" between the top (회초/*hoicho*) and the bottom (회말/*hoimal*) of the seventh inning. Find a video of "Take Me Out to the Ball Game" online, and see if you can fill in the blanks below.[6] After you have tried a few times, look for the complete lyrics online and see how well you did.

Take me out to the _________ _________,
Take me out with the _________.
Buy me some _________ and _________ Jacks,
I _________ _________ if I never get back,
Cause it's root, root, root for the _________ _________,
If they don't _________ it's a shame.
For it's _________, _________, _________ _________, you're _________,
At the old _________ _________.

"Who's on first" is an old vaudeville comedy "routine" performed by Abbott and Costello. Here is the joke: the tall man (Abbott) tells us that the names of the first baseman, second baseman, and third baseman are "Who," "What," and "I Don't Know." The short man (Costello) doesn't understand that those are their names and thinks that "who" and "what" are relative pronouns (누구/*nugu*, 무엇/*mueot*)

6) youtube.com/watch?v=qscED3psy_U; youtube.com/watch?v=HnHV5FaqvEs

and that "I don't know" is just a phrase indicating lack of knowledge (몰아요/*molayo*). There is confusion between questions and statements as well.

Again, find an online video for Abbot and Costello's "Who's on First," and listen to it.[7] See if you can identify the names of the pitcher, the catcher, the right fielder, the center fielder, the left fielder, and the shortstop. You might even find a Korean version of this routine.

Look on the internet for various opinions about Beyoncé's performance of "Formation" at the 2016 Super Bowl halftime show. Discuss what you think this shows about American society.

7) youtube.com/watch?v=RatKhtboq2E; youtube.com/watch?v=kTcRRaXV-fg

Topic 8

Sports in America – II

The Super Bowl, March Madness (see the next chapter), the World Series. These are three sporting events that show athletes at the highest levels of skill. Of course, those athletes usually begin to develop their skills when they are young boys and girls. They are not alone, as most Americans play some sort of organized sport when they are young. According to one report,

> Sixty-nine percent of girls and 75 percent of boys in the United States participate in organized and team sports, according to the 2008 report titled "Go Out and Play: Participation in Team or Organized Sports" conducted by the Women's Sports Foundation. Between 2006 and 2007, approximately 7,342,910 boys and girls participated in high school sports. While youth participation in sports continues to rise, 15 percent have never participated in sports.[1)]

Sports let young children play with their friends and make new friends. At their best, sports help children keep

1) Kay Uzoma, "How Many Youth Participate in Sports in the U.S.?" *Livestrong.com* 13 Dec 2015. livestrong.com/article/373329-how-many-youth-participate-in-sports-in-the-u-s/

physically fit, learn teamwork, and just have fun. These days, youth sports are often for the whole family, as parents come out to watch their children play and support their children. On many weekends in the fall and the spring, for instance, cities will host youth soccer tournaments for teams from elementary-age to high-school age. The players will come with their parents and stay at local hotels and eat at local restaurants, often with the whole team and all the parents.

Other sports organizations offer similar events. One drawback for some people is that sports participation can be expensive, so sometimes children from less economically fortunate families cannot participate on teams that travel. Fortunately, many towns and cities have local leagues, and there is a basketball hoop in nearly every park and on every playground in America. It is also easy to find free tennis courts that are open to the public.

Young people have many opportunities for sports participation. Indeed, they can just gather with neighborhood friends and start a game of baseball or soccer.

Q : From the following list, what do you think are the three most popular sports and recreational activities in which American young people ages 7-17 participate? Notice that some are team sports and some are individual sports or activities.

Volleyball, Tennis, Swimming, Softball, Soccer, Running/Jogging, Hiking, Football, Fishing, Exercise

Walking, Bowling, Billiards, Bicycle Riding, Basketball, Baseball, Aerobics (see the end of the chapter for the answer)

There are many national youth sports organizations. Baseball and softball are very popular, and several national organizations support youth baseball leagues: Little League (littleleague.org); Babe Ruth (baberuthleague.org); Pony Baseball (pony.org); for older youth, there is American Legion Baseball (legion.org/baseball). Another youth sports organization is Pop Warner (popwarner.com).

Q : Which sports does Pop Warner oversee? Another organization is the Amateur Athletic Union, or AAU (aausports.org). What sports does it oversee? Search through the internet for other youth sports organizations in the U.S. Is there an organization for hockey? For swimming? For rodeo? Can you think of other sports?

Unfortunately, the competitive aspect of American culture sometimes overwhelms common sense in sports. We can see the attitude that places winning above all else in this quotation attributed to Vince Lombardi, a famous American football coach for whom the NFL championship trophy is named (the Lombardi Trophy): "Winning isn't everything; it's the only thing." When that attitude infects youth sports, the children stop having fun.

Grantland Rice, a famous American newspaper sports writer, gave a better way of looking at it when he wrote, "It's not that you won or lost but how you played the game." The codes of conduct (below) follow this spirit of good sportsmanship. Notice also that Rice emphasizes the importance of the game for the players not for their parents or other spectators. Perhaps this is another sign of the complicated ways in which Americans (like most people, perhaps) have ideals of sportsmanship in athletics that they do not always follow.

Q : What do you think that American youth (the players themselves) think is most important about playing a sport? What is second? Third? (See the end of the chapter for the answer.)

To win

To have fun

To stay in shape

To play as part of a team

To do something I am good at

To learn new or improve my skills

The different emphases on having fun and winning are exemplified by the different kinds of youth programs available in the U.S. Those programs can be divided into "recreational" and "competitive" programs. The former usually emphasize having fun and developing skills; the latter usually emphasize winning. The latter might also emphasize having fun, but they may emphasize that the best way to have fun is to win, to prove that your team is better than the other team.

Q : Who often emphasizes winning more than having fun?

The answer to the last questions is, of course, "Adults, the parents and the coaches." One of the main reasons children give for dropping out of a sport is that it was no longer fun, and sometimes it is no longer fun because the adults yell at the children and the referees. Sometimes, the adults even engage in violent behavior.

There has been so much bad adult behavior in youth sports that most sports now have codes of conduct that parents and coaches must sign. Here are two examples:

The first example is from AYSO (American Youth Soccer Organization):[2)]

- Support your child.
- Always be positive.

---

2) AYSO, "Codes of Conduct — Be a Good Sport." ayso.org/For_Families/parents_abc.htm#3

- Be enthusiastic and supportive.
- Reinforce positive behavior.
- Let coaches coach and refs ref. Coaches and referees are usually parents. They volunteer their time to help make your child's youth soccer experience a positive one. They need your support, too. What coaches and referees don't need is your help in coaching from the sidelines. So please refrain from coaching during games and practices. Referees are not the "bad guys." They are volunteers, too, and need your support and encouragement. Treat them and their calls fairly and respectfully.

The second example is from Pop Warner, an organization that oversees youth football and cheer and dance. This is from their "Adult Code of Conduct":[3]

- S1: In order to uphold the goals of Pop Warner and ensure that all participants have the benefit of a safe and fun learning environment, all parents, guardians and other adults and attendees of Pop Warner events, . . . must behave . . . in a respectful, courteous and sportsmanlike manner at all times.
- S2: Any adult who is using alcohol, tobacco or non-prescription drugs and/or appears intoxicated at a Pop Warner event, and/or who is flagrantly

3) Pop Warner, "Adult Code of Conduct." popwarner.com/AssetFactory.aspx?did=153

rude, attempts to intimidate, verbally abuse, heckles, taunts, ridicules, boos, throws objects and/or uses vulgarity or profane language/ gestures with an official, coach, volunteer, staff member, participant or other event attendee, must receive a verbal warning and/or be asked to leave a Pop Warner event. . . . The adult's children may also be removed from the event. Any adult who commits one of the above stated offenses a second time, will be banned from any and all Pop Warner events for a minimum period of one year . . . , and their children may also be removed from the program(s) for that time period.

- S3: Any adult who physically or verbally assaults an official, coach, volunteer, staff member or participant or threatens grave bodily harm may be banned from any and all Pop Warner events at a minimum for one year from the date of the offense, and their children may also be removed from any and all Pop Warner programs . . . [I]if the individual commits another offense of the adult code of conduct, the individual will be permanently banned from any and all Pop Warner events.

High School Sports

Almost every high school in the U.S. sponsors multiple sports.

Q : Look at this website for a high school in Oxford, Mississippi: www.oxfordsd.org/page/863. How many different sports for boys and for girls can you find on that website?

High School sports are governed by the National Federation of State High School Associations (NFSHSA), which establishes rules that all high schools must follow. These rules might include limiting the amount of practice time so that students still have time to do their homework, establishing a minimum grade point average (GPA) for participation, and setting guidelines for parental behavior.[4)]

For each boys' sport there is a girls' sport, so both boys and girls have many opportunities for participation. In the 1950s, 60s, and much of the 70s, girls had many fewer opportunities to participate in organized sports than did boys. Then, in 1972 the federal government passed a law called "Title IX" ("IX" is nine in Roman numerals). Title IX requires gender equity (equality) in any educational program that receives money from the federal government. It is explained by a history website like this:

> Many people have never heard of Title IX. Most people who know about Title IX think it applies only to sports, but athletics is only one of 10 key areas addressed by the law. These areas are: Access to Higher Education, Career Education, Education for Pregnant

4) nfhs.org/HomePage

and Parenting Students, Employment, Learning Environment, Math and Science, Sexual Harassment, Standardized Testing and Technology.[5)]

Because schools were required to have an equal number of boys and girls sports teams, many other organizations developed to include teams for both genders. Look at the Pop Warner website again. Pop Warner now sponsors more than one sport. Originally, it sponsored only one.

Q : Which of the sports do you think was originally sponsored?

High school sports are very popular, and local newspapers, especially in small towns, report an all sorts of high school sporting events in the area. One big event in many localities are the high school football games on Friday nights in the fall. Indeed, a very popular television show about high school football in Texas, where it is very, very popular, was called *Friday Night Lights*. It ran from 2006 to 2011 and received several major awards.

Q : Here are two lists, the ten most popular girls' high school sports, and the ten most popular boys' high school sports. Which do you think are the most popular? Why? Perhaps you might gather

5) "History of Title IX." titleix.info/History/History-Overview.aspx

in groups to discuss this. (The answers are at the end of the chapter.)

Top 10 Girls High School Sports	Top 10 Boys High School Sports
Basketball	Baseball
Competitive Spirit Squads	Basketball
Cross Country	Cross Country
Lacrosse	Football
Soccer	Golf
Softball - Fast Pitch	Soccer
Swimming and Diving	Swimming and Diving
Tennis	Tennis
Track and Field	Track and Field
Volleyball	Wrestling

Sometimes, high school sports get a little too much emphasis. In 2012, the town of Allen, Texas spent 60 million dollars on a football stadium for their high school football team. That is about 68,000,000,000 won (6백8십억/*6baek 8shipeok*).[6] In an instance of what might be called "poetic justice," the stadium was closed two years after it opened because cracks in the stadium revealed that it was structurally unsound (dangerous).[7]

6) Abby Ellin, "$60 Million High School Football Stadium," ABC News 24 August 2012. abcnews.go.com/blogs/business/2012/08/60-million-high-school-football-stadium/

7) Marcus Murphree, "$60M Allen Football Stadium deemed 'Not Safe,' Will Close This Season," *Dallas News* May 2014. http://www. dallasnews.com/news/news/2014/05/19/60m-allen-football-stadium-deemed-not-

FOR FURTHER CONSIDERATION

Here are examples of both competitive and recreational baseball and softball programs from the web page of the Parks and Recreation Department of Brainerd, Minnesota. What differences do you notice between the descriptions of recreational and competitive teams?

- Mustang Baseball. This is a highly *competitive* baseball program coached by volunteers who focus on teaching the fundamentals of baseball. Uniforms are provided for players in this league. Boys and girls ages 9 - 10.
- Bronco Baseball. This is a highly *competitive* baseball program coached by volunteers who teach the fundamentals of baseball. Uniforms are provided for players in this league. Boys and girls ages 11 - 12.
- Pony Baseball. This is a highly *competitive* baseball program coached by volunteers who teach advanced offensive and defensive skills. Uniforms are provided for players in this league. Boys and girls ages 13 - 14.
- Petite Softball. This is a *competitive* pitching machine league where players work on basic skills, especially hitting. Fundamentals are taught by volunteer coaches. Uniforms are provided for players in this league. Girls ages 8 - 10.

---

safe-will-close-this-season

- Junior Softball. Basic fundamentals of *competitive* slow-pitch softball are taught by volunteer coaches. Players pitch to batters in this league. Uniforms are provided for players in the league. Girls ages 11 - 13.
- Senior Softball. This is a highly *competitive* slow-pitch league. Advanced skills in offense and defense are taught by volunteer coaches. Uniforms are provided for players in this league. Girls ages 14 - 17.
- Lil Buckaroo's T-Ball. This is a *recreational* league where boys and girls are introduced to T-ball. Parents, guardians or a teen-age sibling are required to help their child or sibling bat and field. Team shirt included! Boys and girls ages 3 and 4.
- Shetland T-Ball. This is a *recreational* league where the players learn to throw, catch, and hit off a tee. Team shirt included! Boys and girls ages 5 and 6.
- Pinto Baseball. A *recreation* aide will pitch underhand to batters, promoting eye/hand coordination and also teach basic skills. Team shirt included! Boys and girls ages 7 and 8.
- Colt Baseball. This is a *non-competitive* pitching machine league where players work on basic skills, especially hitting and fielding. Team shirt included! Boys and girls ages 9 - 12.

For another example of the difference between youth sports that emphasize recreation and those that emphasize competition, compare the websites for the main youth soccer (known as "football" to most of the rest of the world) organizations. One is the American Youth Soccer Organization, or AYSO (ayso.org); the other is U.S. Youth Soccer (usyouthsoccer.org). Compare the images on each home page and connect those images to the varying emphases on tryouts, tournaments, and championships. One organization has tryouts in order to balance the skill levels of players on each team, and every child who tries out is placed on a team. The other organization has competitive tryouts in which only the most skilled players are accepted on a team; many young people are disappointed because they are not placed on a team. Which organization conducts the most competitive tryouts?

Answers to some of the QUESTIONS

Most popular sports and recreational activities for young people ages 7-17 (in millions): [8)]

	Ages 7-17	Ages 7-11	Ages 12-17
Swimming	16.4	8.3	8.1
Bicycle Riding	13.2	6.8	6.4
Bowling	12.4	6.0	6.4

8) From *Statistical Abstract of the United States: 2012* published by the U.S. Census Bureau www2.census.gov/library/publications/2011/ compendia/statab/131ed/2012-statab.pdf

	Ages 7-17	Ages 7-11	Ages 12-17
Basketball	11.3	4.8	6.5
Exercise Walking	9.1	3.6	5.5
Soccer	8.3	5.1	3.2
Running/Jogging	7.7	2.7	5.0
Hiking	6.8	3.0	3.8
Baseball	6.7	4.0	2.7
Fishing	6.6	3.1	3.5
Football	5.1	1.7	3.4
Volleyball	4.4	1.3	3.1
Softball	4.0	1.8	2.2
Billiards	3.4	1.1	2.3
Aerobics	3.3	1.3	2.0
Tennis	2.9	1.4	1.5

In 1989, Michigan State researchers Martha Ewing and Vern Seefeldt studied 28,000 boys and girls around the country and asked, "Why do you play sports?" The most frequent answer was "for fun"; the next two answers were "to do something I'm good at" and "to improve my skills." "Winning" was not even in the the top 10.[9)]

9) Mark Hyman, "A Survey of Youth Sports Finds Winning Isn't the Only Thing," *NY Times* 30 January 2010. nytimes.com/2010/01/31/sports/31youth.html

Most Popular High School Sports:[10]

Girls	Boys
1. Track and Field - Outdoor 478,726	1. Football - 11-Player 1,083,617
2. Basketball 432,176	2. Track and Field - Outdoor 578,632
3. Volleyball 429,504	3. Basketball 541,479
4. Soccer 375,681	4. Baseball 486,567
5. Softball - Fast Pitch 364,103	5. Soccer 432,569
6. Cross Country 221,616	6. Wrestling 258,208
7. Tennis 182,876	7. Cross Country 250,981
8. Swimming and Diving 166,838	8. Tennis 157,240
9. Competitive Spirit Squads 125,763	9. Golf 148,823
10. Lacrosse 84,785	10. Swimming and Diving 137,087

Not every high school offers every sport. Here are the top ten girls and boys sports by the number of high schools that offer the sport:[11]

10) The National Federation of State High School Associations, *2014-15 High School Athletics Participation Survey*. nfhs.org/ParticipationStatistics/PDF/2014-15_Participation_Survey_Results.pdf

11) The National Federation of State High School Associations, 2014-15 *High School Athletics Participation Survey*. nfhs.org/ParticipationStatistics/

Girls	Boys
1. Basketball 17,653	1. Basketball 18,072
2. Track and Field - Outdoor 16,309	2. Track and Field - Outdoor 16,358
3. Volleyball 15,534	3. Baseball 15,899
4. Softball - Fast Pitch 15,115	4. Cross Country 14,635
5. Cross Country 14,287	5. Football - 11 Player 14,154
6. Soccer 11,502	6. Golf 13,528
7. Tennis 10,099	7. Soccer 11,838
8. Golf 9,824	8. Wrestling 10,597
9. Swimming and Diving 7,526	9. Tennis 9,725
10. Competitive Spirit Squads 5,358	10. Swimming and Diving 7,156

There may be various reasons for the popularity of different sports, including the emphasis a sport gets in college and professional leagues. Football, for instance, is America's most popular spectator sport, watched by millions of people every weekend (college games are usually on Saturday, and professional games are usually on Sunday, but there are many exceptions to this as well), and that popularity

---

PDF/2014-15_Participation_Survey_Results.pdf

transfers to high school participation rates for boys. Track and field, however, is not a very popular spectator sport except for a few events during the Olympics. What football and track and field have in common is that both have room for many students on the teams. About 77 students play football at an average high school, although only 11 can play at one time; most of the participants are boys, but sometimes a girl will join the team. About 29 girls and 35 boys participate in outdoor track and field at an average high school. About 24 girls and 30 boys play basketball at an average high school. About 29 girls participate in volleyball at the average high school.[12)]

12) The National Federation of State High School Associations, *2014-15 High School Athletics Participation Survey*. nfhs.org/ParticipationStatistics/PDF/2014-15_Participation_Survey_Results.pdf

Topic 9

Sports in America — III

College Sports

Sports and recreation continue to be an important part of student life in colleges and universities. U.S. colleges and universities have many college-sponsored athletic teams. The annual NCAA Basketball Tournament, or March Madness, is one of the most popular collegiate spectator sports. In the autumn, college football is very popular, and is usually broadcast all day on Saturdays. As noted above, Friday nights are for high school football, but Saturday afternoons are the traditional time for college football games.

Many college sports are regulated by the National Collegiate Athletic Association, or NCAA (pronounced "N-C-double-A"). The NCAA is divided into three different "divisions." Division I sports can award many athletic scholarships. Division II sports can award a more limited number of athletic scholarships. Division III sports cannot award any athletic scholarships. Usually, the best players in any sport attend Division I schools. To learn more about the NCAA and collegiate sports, look at the website at www.ncaa.com.

The NCAA oversees *intercollegiate* sports. Those are sports with matches between teams representing two different colleges or universities: "inter" means "between," so these sports are between two different colleges. NCAA sponsored sports are called *varsity* sports. Those varsity sports have paid professional coaches and are funded primarily by the university athletic budget. The emphasis on varsity sports, especially football and basketball, is indicated by the fact that in 39 of the 50 United States, the basketball or football coach at the main public university is the highest paid public employee in the state.[1]

In 2016, the highest paid collegiate football coach in America was Nick Saban of the University of Alabama, who earned 7.09 million dollars. Jim Harbaugh of the University of Michigan was close behind at 7.004 million dollars.[2] The highest paid collegiate basketball coaches were John Calipari of the University of Kentucky, who made about 6.36 million dollars, and Mike Krzyzewski (pronounced "shi-shev-ski") of Duke University, who made about 6.04 million dollars.[3] For comparison, the highest paid president of a public university, Renu Khator of the University of Houston, made 1.3 million dollars, while the highest paid president of a private university, Lee Bollinger of Columbia

---

1) "The Highest Paid Public Employee in Every State," *24/7 Wall St* 20 September 2016. 247wallst.com/special-report/2016/09/20/the-highest-paid-public-employee-in-every-state/

2) Jimmie Kaylor, "Who Are the Highest-Paid College Football Coaches in 2016?" *Sports CheatSheet* 12 October 2016. cheatsheet.com/sports/highest-paid-college-football-coaches-2016.html/.

3) Jason Alsher, "The 7 Highest-Paid College Basketball Coaches," *Sports CheatSheet* 17 January 2017. cheatsheet.com/sports/the-top-7-highest-paid-coaches-in-college-basketball.html/.

University, made 4.6 million dollars.[4][5] The President of the United States makes 400 *thousand* dollars per year, with additional compensation of 169 thousand dollars for travel, expenses, and entertainment. Clearly, Americans have decided that their most valuable public employees are coaches.

Q : What sort of American values do you think coaches' salaries might represent?

Besides varsity sports, another kind of intercollegiate sports are *club* sports. These sports are not sponsored by the NCAA, and they do not have fulltime professional coaches. The teams are organized and funded primarily by the students themselves, although the college or university might contribute some money. The student members themselves establish practice and game schedules. These club teams compete against club teams from other colleges and universities. While the institution will pay for travel for varsity teams, club teams usually pay for their own transportation.

Finally, colleges also sponsor *intramural* sports and *recreational* activities for the general student population. These activities are for students within the college or university:

4) Monica Wang, "The 10 Public University Presidents With The Highest Pay," *Forbes Online*. 17 July 2016. forbes.com/sites/monicawang/2016/07/17/the-10-public-university-presidents-with-the-highest-pay/.

5) Susan Adams, "The Highest-Paid Private College Presidents," *Forbes Online* 7 December 2015. Web. forbes.com/sites/susanadams/2015/12/07/the-highest-paid-private-college-presidents/.

"intra" means "within," and "mural" means "walls"; thus, these sports are organized within the walls of the institution. For team sports, students will form teams themselves with their friends, and they will play against other teams organized by other students from the same college or university.

Here is a list of intramural sports from a typical mid-sized American university, James Madison University (JMU) in Harrisonburg, Virginia:[6]

> Battleship, Basketball (3-on-3 Outdoor), Basketball (5-on-5), Dodgeball, Disc Golf, Field Hockey, Flag Football (4-on-4), Flag Football (7-on-7), Floor Hockey, Futsal, Indoor Lacrosse, Racquetball, Sand Volleyball (4-on-4), Soccer (Indoor), Soccer (Outdoor), Softball, Street Hockey, Summer Soccer, Team Handball, Tennis, Ultimate Frisbee, Volleyball, Wallyball.

Q : Some of these sports are rather unusual. What is battleship? What is wallyball? What other sports seem interesting? Many colleges and universities, especially in the northern part of the U.S., sponsor intramural broomball. What is that?

Besides intramural sports, JMU offers its students many other opportunities for recreational activities and physical

6) jmu.edu/recreation/index.shtml

fitness. Those opportunities include adventure and challenge courses like rock climbing, aquatics, fitness and personal training, group exercise, nutrition, and wellness and massage.

One collegiate tradition that usually revolves around a football game is called "Homecoming." Not every college or university has a football team, so often another sporting event will be the center of the homecoming celebration, which usually lasts for three or four days, often beginning the Friday before the big game, and continuing to the following Saturday and Sunday. Homecoming is a time for the school's alumni and alumnae (or just "alums": graduates of a school) to come "home" to visit their old *alma mater* (college from which they graduated). Besides the game, there are often many other events such as a parade, a golf tournament, a dance, and/or a bonfire.

As you can see, Americans enjoy sports at various levels as spectators and as participants. Indeed, there are many opportunities for organized sports activities even after people pass out of youth into middle ages and older. Many Americans enjoy golf, and greens fees are often much less expensive than they are in other countries. Many cities and towns in the U.S. have a "parks and recreation" department, or something with a similar name. Those departments sponsor youth sports, like the baseball and softball teams in Brainerd, Minnesota noted above. There are many opportunities for adults as well, even older adults. City softball leagues are popular throughout the country, for both men's, women's, and co-ed teams. The Brainerd Parks and Recreation

Department, for instance, sponsors nine different recreational softball leagues including one for the "Ageless Wonders," which is for ages 55 and older.

The Parks and Recreation Department for Staunton, Virginia, offers various recreational and sports activities for adults as well. Under "Athletics and Fitness," it offers men's flag football, co-ed futsal, co-ed volleyball, a walking club, and full-body fitness. Under "Health and Wellness," activities like Walk with a Doc, Morning Warm-ups, Vinyasa Yoga, Sunrise Yoga, Yoga for Every Body, and Therapeutic Qi Gong, among others. To get some exercise through "Dance and Music," people can try Intro to Scottish Country Dance, Just a Swingin'—East Coast Single Swing (beginners), Still Swingin'—East Coast Single Swing (advanced), American Style Waltz, Line Dance, Advanced Line Dance, and Country English Dance. And those are only the fall offerings. The other three seasons will have their activities as well.[7)]

March Madness

College varsity sports, especially Division I basketball and football, are very popular spectator sports. One of the most popular televised college sporting events, commonly known as "March Madness," is the National Collegiate Athletic Association Division I Men's Basketball Tournament.

---

7) *Staunton Parks and Recreation Fall 2016 Brochure.* Staunton, Virginia: City of Staunton, 2016.

The college basketball season begins around the middle of November and continues through the second week of March (while the Korean academic years runs from March to December, the American academic year runs from September to June). The tournament takes place over about three and a half weeks from the middle of March to the beginning of April.

The tournament begins with Selection Sunday, which was March 13 in 2016, the year we will use as an example. On Selection Sunday, a committee of experts selects 68 teams to participate in the tournament. Eight of those teams meet in four play-in games on the Tuesday and Wednesday after Selection Sunday (March 15 and 16 in 2016). The four winners of those games join the other 60 teams who were chosen in the tournament "bracket." Those 64 teams are divided into four regions with 16 teams each. The winner of each region goes to the "Final Four" to decide the champion for the year. The entire 2016 bracket is on the NCAA website.[8] Looking at the bracket will help you follow the explanation below.

After the play-in games, there are 32 games in the first round on the next Thursday and Friday (March 17 and 18), and 16 games in the second round on Saturday and Sunday (March 19 and 20). The third round, called the "Sweet Sixteen," takes place on the next Thursday and Friday (March 24 and 25). The next round, called the "Elite Eight,"

---

8) "2016 Division I Men's Basketball Championship Official Bracket." ncaa.com/interactive-bracket/basketball-men/d1/2016

takes place on Saturday and Sunday (March 26 and 27).

After the Elite Eight, there are only four teams left, and they play two semi-final games as "The Final Four" on the following Saturday (April 2). The championship game is played the next Tuesday (April 4). In 2016, Villanova University beat the University of North Carolina in the championship game. The NCAA website lists every champion since the tournament began in 1939.[9)]

Many people in the U.S. fill out a bracket, picking the winners of each game before the tournament begins. President Barack Obama made his picks every year and shared his bracket with the nation. You can compare the NCAA bracket with President Obama's picks to see how well he did by searching the internet for "Obama 2016 March Madness Bracket." You will find that he also filled out a bracket for the women's tournament, which takes place at about the same time as the men's tournament. While the women's tournament is not as widely followed and does not inspire as much "madness" as the men's tournament, it is also very exciting.

Often, friends will have a tournament contest to see who can pick the most winners. Sometimes, gambling is involved. That is, each person contributes a small sum of money, and the person who picks the most winners gets the money as a reward. Often, people who work in an office or other business together will have an "office pool" of some

---

9) "Men's' Basketball Championship History." ncaa.com/history/basketball-men/d1

sort. Almost all of the games can be watched via live streaming on the internet, and sometimes people watch the games while they are "working" at the office. According to some estimates, the lost productivity in watching basketball games during March Madness cost American businesses almost 4 billion dollars in 2016. Nonetheless, some management experts advise to let employees enjoy the tournament because it is good for office morale and creates camaraderie (what Koreans might call *jeong*—정/情).[10] Many online sites, such as ESPN, let people submit brackets electronically and give prizes to the winners.

Anyone interested in why the tournament is called March *Madness* might get online and search for videos on "March Madness Buzzer Beaters." A "buzzer-beater" is a shot that comes at the end of a game to win the game when the winning team was behind by one or two points just before the shot. When a player makes a buzzer-beater to win the game, the players and the fans go wild. They get crazy: that is the madness.[11]

FOR FURTHER CONSIDERATION

Go to one of these college or university websites and find out about their varsity, club, and intramural

10) "Employers Brace for March Madness," *Challenger, Gray, and Christmas, Inc.* 8 March 2016. www.challengergray.com/press/press-releases/employers-brace-march-madness

11) For an example, see "March Madness Buzzer Beaters and Game Winners (2015-16)." youtube.com/watch?v=GuD5QIOYR6o

opportunities: Davidson College, Appalachian State University, University of Minnesota-Morris, Montana State University, Coppin State University, Oberlin College, or some other college or university that you would like to explore. Get a list of colleges and universities with which your university has exchange programs and look for their varsity, club, and intramural sports and recreational activities.

Choose one of the schools above and find out about their homecoming through an internet search. Perhaps you can form small groups and report back to the class about what you find.

If your class is during spring semester, class members might fill out brackets that they find on the NCAA or ESPN website to see who can pick the most winners.

Topic 10

Images of Women in American Popular Culture

Images of women pervade American popular culture, especially in its consumerism. Television commercials make use of gender depictions, male and female, to sell many different products. One such commercial was a Fiat 500 Abarth commercial that aired during the 2012 Super Bowl. That commercial was rated as the most popular commercial on the nfl.com website by viewers. Other websites that ask for viewer responses to the commercials did not rate it so highly. In fact, some sites that are used primarily by women showed some viewers to be highly offended by the commercial.

The commercial begins with a somewhat tired-looking man walking down a city street with a cup of coffee in his hand. He looks like an office worker. He notices something in the street and turns his head to stare. The viewer, sharing the man's visual perspective, sees a beautiful woman in tall spiked heels bending over and rubbing her ankle. She has a fairly short skirt, black with red trim, and shapely legs. Because of her position, the video also emphasizes her buttocks and her breasts, two of the most frequent anatomical foci for sexualizing women. She suddenly turns her head and catches the man and the television viewers staring at her.

She shouts something in a non-English language—Italian. Most American viewers would not be able to understand what she says, but many would recognize that she speaks Italian. She speaks several more times, always in Italian, except for the last time she speaks.

The camera shot switches back to the man, who turns his eyes away in apparent embarrassment. The woman stands up and strides toward the man, again speaking in an angry, scolding tone. As she approaches him, viewers see that she is taller than he is, and the camera angle, which puts the woman in the foreground and diminishes the man by distance and perspective, makes her seem even more imposing. When she reaches him, she slaps his face, and he backs up against a light post. She then grabs him by his tie, speaking loudly to him again.

She then says something in a softer tone and moves closer to him, suddenly seeming almost affectionate, even romantic. She puts one hand on his chest and says something softly again. She caresses his cheek and whispers in his ear. She looks into his eyes, and he nods his head, although he seems not to understand anything she is saying. She dips her finger into his coffee, which has some foam on it, perhaps whipped cream. As the camera follows her foam-covered finger toward her lips, a dollop of the foam slips from her finger and falls on her breasts, where the camera pauses. Both the man and the woman look at the dollop of white cream on her breast. She touches the cream remaining on her fingers to his lips. He closes his eyes, as she leans in for what seems like it will be a kiss, and the viewer notices a scorpion tattoo on the back of her neck. His face fills the whole screen in a very close shot. His eyes are closed, and his mouth puckers for the expected kiss.

The shot changes, moving back out, and the man is about to kiss the window of an automobile. It is a black car. With red trim. And a scorpion symbol, like the tattoo on the woman's neck. The viewer then hears the woman's voice-over in English with a European accent. It seems to be the voice of the woman from the commercial. She says, "The Fiat 500 Abarth. You'll never forget the first time you see one."

The scene then shifts to the automobile being filmed as it is driven rapidly through the city streets, then to the inside of the car, where a man's hand quickly and authoritatively moves the gear shift. The final shot of the commercial is again from the interior of the car, looking out at the man with the coffee as his face holds an enraptured smile. He is in love with the car.

It is a very skillfully-made commercial, but it reflects various issues of how women are portrayed in American media.

As you think about the Fiat commercial and other depictions of women in the media, keep in mind key points from Sheri Kathleen Cole's important 1999 essay titled "The Pornographic Ideology of Music Videos."[1] Cole

1) *Enculturation* 2.2 (Spring 1999). Available online at enculturation.net/2_2/cole/index.html.

identifies the following "pornographic" qualities of MTV music videos. The Fiat commercial, with its background music, is itself a brief version of a music video.[2)] Some important terms that are very useful in analyzing media images of women are "objectification" (undercutting a woman's humanity by turning her into an "object" of male pleasure), "commodification" (treating women as "commodities," things that can be bought and sold), the "gaze" (the male viewing position that controls how we see the women depicted), and "bits and pieces" (focusing on women's body parts rather than the person as a whole, often parts such as buttocks, breasts, and legs). Here are some of Cole's most important ideas:

- What effect do images of women have on the female fans who follow popular music groups and consume music videos? Because pornography harms real women by both its impact and creation of sexual stereotypes, music videos repeat this ideological content and harm by replicating these images.
- The feminist analysis of pornography is grounded in an image's use of violence against women, degrading poses, objectification of women's bodies (or body parts), and the reduction of women's status to that of sexual object available for the accessibility or conquest by the (male) viewer.

2) The song used in the commercial is "Smokescreen" by Willis. youtube.com/watch?v=xfpPE49uUWw

- Commodification of sexuality is central to the creation of most music videos. Sexualized representations of women in videos partially define sex for the larger culture, viewers, and popular music fans. And the "sex" of pornography and music video is the objectification of women, the sexually explicit depiction of women's subordination, and the eroticization of (female) submission and (male) dominance.
- [Media use] the pornographic convention of "bits and pieces" as defined by Annette Kuhn. The camera emphasizes one particular body part of a woman in order to sexualize that "piece" of her, a gesture of dehumanization because one part of the woman is made to stand for the whole person. The model, quite literally, is her breasts, her buttocks, and even her hands or feet—whatever body part the camera chooses to linger on and sexualize.
- "The gaze": a moving camera . . . leads the viewer's gaze along the woman's body, stopping momentarily on whatever part the director means to emphasize. . . . All viewers are taught to see these videos through the "male gaze."
- Women in the videos are rarely portrayed with the "power" to look directly into the camera, to meet its *gaze* or the gaze of the "viewer" on the other side. The male position as voyeur, therefore, is rarely challenged or rejected. The "caught unawares"

convention creates a world in which women are not only available for sexual access and use, but are willing, as well.

- The feminist argument [is] that pornography is the colonization of women for privatized and unlimited sexual access by men.
- Whoever controls the "eye"—whether that is defined as the camera, the gaze, or the image—also controls the "victim"—the subject, the photographer's fetish object, most notably women.

As Cole notes in the first point above, images of women in media can have negative effects on female viewers, especially young women and girls. *Media Smarts: Canada's Centre for Digital and Media Literacy* focuses on these effects in two informative web page. Here are some key points from "Body Image—Girls":[3]

- Images of female bodies are everywhere, with women and girls—and their body parts—selling everything from food to cars.
- The causes, some analysts say, are economic: by presenting a physical ideal that is difficult to achieve and maintain the cosmetic and diet industries are assured continual growth and profits.
- Marketers know that girls and women who are

3) mediasmarts.ca/body-image/body-image-girls

insecure about their bodies are more likely to buy beauty products, new clothes, and diet aids, and a whole media industry has developed around fueling body dissatisfaction.

- Research links exposure to images of thin, young, air-brushed female bodies to depression, loss of self-esteem and unhealthy eating habits in girls and young women: in one study half of girls ages 16-21 said they would undergo surgery to improve their bodies.
- The real tragedy [. . .] is that many girls internalize these stereotypes, and judge themselves by the beauty industry's standards.
- It is essential that girls and young women develop a critical understanding of the constructed nature of media representations of women's bodies and the reasons why these images are perpetuated.

Here are some key points from the other web page, "Media and Girls":[4]

- Women represent 49 per cent of humanity while female characters make up only 32 per cent of the main characters on TV.
- Girls' confidence frequently drops in the pre-teen years as they begin to base their feelings of self-worth

4) mediasmarts.ca/gender-representation/women-and-girls/media-and-girls

more and more heavily on appearance and weight.

- Girls are surrounded by images of female beauty that are unrealistic and unattainable.
- The hypersexualization of very young girls, most notably in fashion and advertising, is a disturbing trend given that these stereotypes make up most of the representations of themselves which girls and women see in the media.
- Young girls are being bombarded with images of sexuality, often dominated by stereotypical portrayals of women and girls as powerless, passive victims.

One other useful source is a short video called "Cause and Effect: How the Media You Consume Can Change Your Life." This video gives some keys facts about media images of women and how they affect girls.[5] These facts include:

- Three of four girls feel depressed, guilty, and shameful after looking through a fashion magazine for three minutes.
- 48% of girls wish they were as skinny as fashion models.
- 31% of girls admit to starving themselves to lose weight.

The following example of a magazine advertisement

5) youtube.com/watch?v=Hv5Z2Xv8iJU

for a popular perfume suggests ways to think critically about women's representations.[6)]

The first thing a person might notice is an attractive blonde woman holding a green apple with a bite taken out of it. Written across the photograph in the same green color as the apple, is the phrase in capital letters "BE DELICIOUS." After that, attention might shift to the green apples piled in the foreground, the upper-case "DKNY" superimposed on the apples, the lower-case explanation that BE DELICIOUS is "the fragrance for women." Unlike the women in the music videos that Sheri Kathleen Cole analyzes, who do not meet the male gaze, the woman in this ad looks

6) Lara Stone by Mikael Jansson. "Lara Stone for Be Delicious DKNY Fragrance." *Designscene* 27 October 2010. Web.

directly at the viewer, returning the gaze. Is that enough to say that this ad avoids the trap of objectification? Perhaps for some.

But let's take a closer look. First, we might ask ourselves at whom the woman is looking.

Q : What position does the viewer take in the little story that this advertisement tells?

Perhaps we should take another step back and consider what story the ad tells. Notice that there is a light shining behind the woman's head. That light around the head is like a halo, which, in western traditions, often indicated holiness, purity, innocence. Thus, one subtle visual aspect of this add suggests the woman is innocent.

Yet, the ad also suggests that innocence has been lost. The woman holds out an apple with a bite out of it.

Q : In what origin story from the Western religious tradition of Christianity does a woman offer a man a fruit?

One of the most obvious allusions of that apple is to the Biblical story of how Adam and Eve lost their innocence and brought sin into the world. Briefly, Adam and Eve were the first two human beings created by God. They lived in a garden, Eden, and God gave them fruit to eat from all of the trees except one. He said they could not eat from the tree of the knowledge of good and evil. In their state of innocence, they knew nothing of evil.

Satan, the devil, took the shape of a talking snake and convinced Eve to eat the fruit from the tree of the knowledge of good and evil. Eve then convinced Adam to eat the fruit. Thus, sin and evil entered the world. That fruit is often depicted as an apple, although the Bible never identifies the particular kind of fruit it was.

Thus, the woman in the advertisement is an image of Eve, and she is tempting Adam with the apple. The viewer is, therefore, in the position of Adam, or of any man who is tempted by a woman. Even female viewers are looking through a man's eyes, with the modern-day Eve looking back at them.

An apple is delicious, and no one would think that offering someone a delicious apple is sinful. But what else is delicious in the ad? Since this is a "fragrance for women," and the smell will be delicious, the very name of the perfume tells women, using the imperative, a command, to be delicious. We like to eat delicious things, like apples.

Q : If the woman is delicious, she should be eaten and enjoyed, the ad tells us. Who will eat her?

The answer to that last question is obvious. While *the*

viewer of the ad is constructed as having a male gaze, the *consumer* of the product will turn herself into the object of that gaze. If the viewer is a woman, she is asked to see herself through the male gaze, as a tempting object for consumption – let's not forget that "to consume" suggests a consumer, someone who buys goods or commodities, but it also means "to eat," even "to devour." The consumer, the one who buys a product (a woman), is also encouraged to be consumed, to be the object of consumption for some interested male. Of course, a man might buy this perfume for some woman in whom he has an interest. Such a gift, of course, again encourages the woman to "be delicious." For whom? For the man who gave her the gift.

Another look at the ad suggests that the woman becomes a sexualized fantasy for the male-constructed viewer. Notice that the woman is wearing a sweater that has slipped from her shoulders, revealing the straps of her brassiere: her clothes are slipping from her. Indeed, other Be Delicious ads show a woman wearing nothing while holding an apple. In this ad, we also notice one other signal from an old Western tradition that this woman is not innocent at all. The woman in the ad does not have the perfect teeth of many models: there is a gap between her two front teeth. For hundreds of years in the West, going at least as far back as Chaucer's Wife of Bath, a gap-toothed woman was considered to be promiscuous.

If one looks closely at the pile of green apples in the foreground of the ad, one of the apples on the right is not an actual apple at all but an apple-shaped perfume bottle in which the fragrance is sold. One side of the bottle is silver, and in that silver side is reflected a famous New York landmark, the Empire State Building. Thus, the phallic skyscraper penetrates the juicy apple that represents the feminine. Some might think that last bit of analysis might go too far, but it is entirely consistent with the other unspoken messages that the advertisement communicates.

Again, this is a very well-made advertisement. It is quite intelligent in its many subtle appeals to the potential consumer. It tells a woman that it is her role to be attractive and available to men. It suggests that the woman who uses this perfume can be like the beautiful woman in the picture. It makes the woman viewing the ad feel inadequate if she is not as beautiful as the woman in the ad. It tells women that one way to compensate for their lack of this woman's beauty is to buy the perfume that makes them delicious to men.

FOR FURTHER CONSIDERATION

Find the Fiat commercial on an internet website like *Youtube.com* and watch it.[7] After watching the commercial, what do you think might be the reason that viewers on nfl.com rated it so highly but other viewers did not? What ideas from Sheri Kathleen Cole and the other sources in

7) youtube.com/watch?v=HrdKr-p3fWc

the chapter can you use in a critique of the commercial? Identify specific points in Cole's essay that can be applied to specific moments in the commercial. Use Cole's analysis to reflect on images that you see in other media besides television commercials: print advertisements, billboards, posters in shop windows, television shows, movies, and music videos, for instance.

This might be a good project: go to the main shopping area near you and look at the advertisements that use images of women. What ideas from Cole and the other sources might you use in thinking about the advertisements?

Find the "extended trailer" for a video titled *Miss Representation* on the internet. You can both practice your English listening skills and learn a lot about women and media in the U.S. The video is part of the work of *The Representation Project* (therepresentationproject.org/). See if you can answer these questions from listening to and watching the video.[8)]

- How many hours a day does the average American teenager spend in media consumption?
- Fill in the blanks: Girls get the message from very early on that what's most important is ______ ______ ______, that their value, their worth

8) youtube.com/watch?v=S5pM1fW6hNs&sns=fb

depends on that, and _______ get the message that this is what's important about girls. We get it from __________; we get it from ________; we get it from _________ shows, video games, everywhere we look, so no matter what else a woman does, no matter what else her achievements, their value still depends on how they ______.

- In the media, women comprise what percent of all writers, directors, producers, cinematographers, and editors?
- Fill in the blanks: A lot of advertising is based on making people feel ________, and feeling ________. The effect is primarily ______________.
- What is the U.S. ranking in terms of women in national legislatures?
- Who says this: "As the most powerful country in the world, if you're not standing for the right values, and the right principles, that's a loss for the world"?
- What movie about sports helped empower young girls? What sport was the movie about? What is the name of the female actor who starred in the movie?[9)]

Some of the media images early in the *Miss Representation* trailer show graphic examples of what Cole and the other

9) Look at seejane.org.

sources have identified in their analyses. Apply those sources to the images from the video.

Of course, the use of sexually suggestive images of women to sell products is not unique to the Unites States. Earlier in this book, we noted LeRoy Ashby's claim that "popular culture has become [America's] leading export." Think about that and locate on the internet a video of a 2012 Toyota Camry commercial from South Korea that featured Kim Tae-hee and the slogan "Have it all."[10] As you watch the commercial, consider Cole's analysis of music videos, particularly what she writes about "bits and pieces." How do that and other ideas presented in this chapter help you reflect on the Camry commercial?

10) youtube.com/watch?v=0kX5VzfTJS0

Topic 11

Images of Men in American Popular Culture

In *American Ways*, Maryanne Kearny Datesman, JoAnn Crandall, and Edward C. Kearny write about America's "Frontier Heritage" as an influence on American beliefs and values.[1] In their discussion, they describe a particular kind of mythologized character that has influenced depictions of masculinity in popular culture. That character is "The Rugged Individual." The qualities of this mythological figure include being physically tough and strong, being skilled with guns (and other weapons), needing no help from others, being alone (unmarried, with no children), protecting others (he may be alone, outside the community but he helps preserve it; he saves it), and defending good against evil.

Datesman, Crandall, and Kearny identify two types of the rugged individual that emerged in the process of "civilizing" the North American continent (through the calling of manifest destiny, no doubt). The first type showed man against the wilderness or nature. That type had to cut down trees to make farm land and to build homes on the frontier, homes that eventually led to towns and cities, to subduing the wilderness for western civilization.

The second manifestation of the rugged individual

1) *American Ways*, 3rd edition (Longman, 2005), 71-78.

was in the struggle of man against man. That struggle was first against Native Americans, or Indians, who were often depicted as violent savages who threatened the expansion of white people into the new land. The struggle then turned to bad men of European heritage who threatened the settlers in the movement westward.

One of the classic film representations of the rugged individual who saved the community by standing up to evil white men was the title character of the 1953 *Shane*. Shane, a mysterious stranger, one day rides into a western town that is being terrorized by an evil rancher and his hired thugs. He gets a job with a farmer and becomes a role model to the young boy. In the climax of the movie, Shane confronts the thugs by himself and defeats them, using, of course, his gun. As the movie closes, Shane rides off alone, back into the wilderness from which he came, while the farmer's son shouts, "Shane, Shane."

Variations on that kind of hero have appeared in hundreds of "westerns" (movies set in the American west, usually in the 19th century, with a cowboy hero) since then. Many of the protagonists (main characters) have not been as purely good as Shane, but often, even those with some bad qualities finally fight on the side of good against evil. One element that has almost entirely disappeared from westerns is a visual reinforcement of the hero's goodness: in early westerns, the good guy wore a white hat, while the bad guys wore black hats.

The rugged individual who fights alone to save the

innocent, to bring some wholeness to the community that he cannot rejoin, has moved from the old west (in the U.S.) to the contemporary city. I would argue that the Korean movie *Ajeossi* shows the influence of the American western hero in contemporary Korean culture, reflecting again the power of American popular culture as an export. Another recent film with Korean roots shows a different blending of cultures. In *Warriors Way*, the martial arts film, with its iconic ninjas, meets the western. The film was directed by the Korean director Lee Seung-mu. It is set in the American west of the 19th century. The main character, very much in the mold of the rugged individual, is played by the Korean actor Jang Dong-gun. His character is, of course, a master of martial arts and employs that mastery to save the town.

The cowboy has always had a strong hold on the popular imagination, especially the imagination of boys. These days, the images are associated more and more with excess violence. There is another, more romantic view of the cowboy that has little to do with violence, however. I will ask you to think about that more romanticized view in two popular songs in the further considerations at the end of the chapter.

The rugged individual has always been identified with violence. Usually, a protagonist in a movie or television drama that features rugged individualism does not want to use violence, but he almost always must use violence. A possible result of that media influence is that the final resolution to a problem is often seen as a violent resolution. Someone (the bad guys) must be punished, even die, for resolution.

One aspect of that attitude toward resolution is an American love affair with guns. Unfortunately, guns often are in the hands of dangerous people.

Q : Do you recognize the person in the photo below? In 2007, he became quite famous (or infamous) in South Korea.

That is Seung Hui Cho (조승희), an emotionally disturbed Korean American who killed 32 people and injured 25 at Virginia Tech University on April 16, 2007. Some Koreans worried that he gave a bad image to the Korean people, but his actions said a lot more about America than about Korea. Mass shootings are committed by white Americans as much as anyone in the U.S.

Before Cho, on April 20, 1999, Dylan Klebold, 18, and Eric Harris, 17, killed 12 students, one teacher and wounded dozens of others at Columbine High School in Littleton, Colorado before killing themselves.

Since Cho's actions, there have been many more horrible gun murders of multiple people. Just a few examples follow.

James Laughner shot Gabrielle Giffords, a congressional representative from Arizona, outside a Tucson shopping mall where she was meeting with constituents January 8, 2011. Six people were killed and another thirteen injured.

James Eagan Holmes killed 12 and injured eight in a movie theater in Aurora, Colorado on July 12, 2012.

Adam Lanza killed 20 children and six adults at Sandy Hook Elementary School in Newtown, Connecticut on December 14, 2012.

Aaron Alexis killed 12 people at the Navy Yard in Washington, DC on September 16, 2013.

Elliot Rodger killed six people in Isla Vista, California on May 23, 2014.

Dylann Roof killed nine people at a prayer meeting at Emanuel African Methodist Episcopal Church in

Charleston, South Carolina on June 17, 2015

Omar Mir Seddique Mateen killed 50 people at the Pulse Night Club in Orlando, Florida on June 12, 2016.

According to an article from CBS News, "Americans are 10 times more likely to be killed by guns than people in other developed countries."[2)]The authors of a recent article in *The American Journal of Medicine* discovered that "U.S. homicide rates were 7.0 times higher than in other high-income countries, driven by a gun homicide rate that was 25.2 times higher." For the 15-24 age range, "the gun homicide rate in the United States was 49.0 times higher." Even though overall suicide rates were about the same as in other developed countries, "firearm-related suicide rates were 8.0 times higher in the United States." Tragically, "unintentional firearm deaths were 6.2 times higher."[3)]

American males are sometimes willing participants in their own casual acceptance of gun violence as somehow normal. Indeed, that acceptance may contribute to what Jaclyn Friedman calls "Toxic Masculinity" in America. Friedman demonstrates her point in yet another connection to sports.

---

2) Robert Preidt, "How U.S. Guns Deatsh Compare to Other Countries," *CBS News* 3 February 2016. cbsnews.com/news/how-u-s-gun-deaths-compare-to-other-countries/

3) Erin Grinshteyn, and David Hemenway, "Violent Death Rates: The U.S. Compared with Other High-income OECD Countries, 2010," *The American Journal of Medicine* 129.8 (March 2016): 266-273. Published online 6 November 2016. amjmed.com/article/S0002-9343(15)01030-X/fulltext; amjmed.com/article/S0002-9343(15)01030-X/pdf

She writes about an incident in which "two young football players in the Ohio town of Steubenville carried the unconscious body of a local girl from party to party, violating her in ways you'd probably prefer not to think about." The boys actually filmed their sexual assaults on the girl and put them online. Friedman describes the town's reaction to the incident:

> Toxic masculinity has its fingerprints all over the Steubenville case. The violence done to the victim was born out of the boys' belief that a) sexually dominating a helpless girl's body made them powerful and cool, and b) there would be no consequences for them because of their status as star athletes. The defense is basing their entire case on it, arguing that this near-(and sometimes totally) unconscious girl's body was the boys' to use because "she didn't affirmatively say no." The football community's response — by which I mean not just the coaches, school, and players, but the entire community of fans — is steeped in the assumptions of toxic masculinity, treating the athletes and the game as more important than some silly girl's right to both bodily autonomy and justice. Steubenville residents have been quick to rally around the team, suggesting that the victim "put herself in a position to be violated" and refusing to talk to police investigating the assault. The two players who cooperated with police were suspended from the football team, while the players accused of the rape have been allowed to play.

> The coach even went so far as to threaten a *New York Times* reporter asking questions about the case. (No surprise there: When it comes to male-dominated sports, toxic masculinity is the rule, not the exception.)[4]

This is just one example of what some people call "rape culture." Indeed, many American men, young and old, are horrified by such behavior, but the willingness to accept or overlook sexual assault was demonstrated during the 2016 American presidential election process when one of the candidates was caught on tape using an obscene term for a woman's vagina while bragging about how he could just "grab them by the pussy." Despite that and numerous other instances of his behaving in insulting ways toward women, Donald Trump was still elected president. Fortunately, there are other men in America who show decency and respect toward woman, men like Barack Obama, the president before Trump who is famous for the respect and love he shows toward his wife Michelle, a woman with impressive educational and professional achievements of her own. As a black woman, she is someone who has overcome both racial and gender prejudice to become a role model for young women throughout the world.

Like the sources identified earlier show media influences on women's self-perception, Jackson Katz, in an essay titled "Men, Masculinities, and Media: Some Introductory

4) "Toxic Masculinity," *The American Prospect* 13 March 2013. prospect.org/article/toxic-masculinity

Notes,"[5] ties the development of toxic masculinity to the media. Here are a few of his key points:

> The climactic scene in *The Wizard of Oz* where Toto pulls back the curtain to reveal a nervous, tragic man pretending to be the Great and Powerful Oz represents more than just a classic moment in American cinematic history. It is also a powerful metaphor for looking at masculinity in a new way: not as a fixed, inevitable, natural state of being, but rather as a projection, a performance, a mask that men often wear to shield our vulnerability and hide our humanity. [. . .]
>
> If you want to understand what's going on with contemporary American masculinities, you have to look at what's going on in the media.
>
> We're not just consumers of these images; we don't simply make our way through the thousands of images we see daily and pick and choose what we like and don't like. These images have a profound impact on who we are, and on our tastes, attitudes, and the kinds of choices we make.[. . .]
>
> While image of women have been thinner and more waifish, images of men have gotten bigger, stronger, more muscular, and more violent. [. . .]
>
> Tough guy posing, even though it's often just an

5) "WCW Research Report," *Wellesley Center for Woman* Spring 1999. biscmi.org/wp-content/uploads/2015/01/Men_Masculinities_and_Media.pdf

> act, also has the effect of keeping men in line. Fed by a constant stream of images informed by the Marlboro Man ethos of the "real man" as a stoic rugged individualist, millions of boys and men learn early on that acting like a man means you don't complain, you don't admit weakness, you don't ever let others see the anxious man behind the curtain. This sort of conditioning starts very young, as does the pressure on boys and young men to compete — in school, in sports, in their social milieu — to live up to their fathers' visions of them as manly men.
>
> But the pretense of omnipotence and invulnerability that is implied by ubiquitous images of physically powerful males [the hypermasculine posture] is not just emotionally stultifying. It also gets a lot of men — and boys — killed [. . .]

Katz's last quoted point about "images of physically powerful males," indicates another growing issue about images of men. Men in media like television and movies have gotten much more muscular in the last thirty years. Just as those media have given unrealistic physical images of women for many years, media also give unrealistic physical images of men.[6] Most men will never achieve the muscular appearance of men in the movies, and the time spent trying to achieve that appearance could be spent reading, learning,

6) Logan Hill, "Building a Bigger Action Hero," *Men's Journal* 18 April 2014. mensjournal.com/magazine/building-a-bigger-action-hero-20140418

and communicating with others. Perhaps those unrealistic images are harmful to some men's self-images. Perhaps they encourage female viewers to consider physical attractiveness to be more important than substantial intellectual or emotional qualities. Perhaps either of those effects are not good for people. What do you think?

Indeed, there are positive models of masculinity in the U.S., but violence is too often glorified, from the X-Men to the Avengers, and even in a sport like American football.

FOR FURTHER CONSIDERATION

Find the following two songs online, listen to them and find the lyrics, then discuss the picture of the late twentieth-century cowboy that they give. What American characteristics do you find in these songs? What signs of the rugged individual do you find? How are these cowboys similar to or different from that mythology of rugged individualism, the western hero?

My Heroes Have Always Been Cowboys (1979)[7)]

Mammas, Don't Let Your Babies Grow Up to Be Cowboys (1978)[8)]

---

7) Two versions: Waylon Jennings (youtube.com/watch?v=qA3oscaTy-U); Willie Nelson (youtube.com/watch?v=OMko5LelBdA)

8) Waylon Jennings and Willie Nelson (youtube.com/watch?v=WyyOqxpcn8g)

A person's "inner light" is their true spirit, the belief or idea or commitment that guides their life. With that knowledge, how would you answer the question in the following image? What is *supposed* to be the right answer?

That image appears as a magazine ad in some American magazines. It is followed, sometimes on the next page, with the next image, which is supposed to be the right answer for "real" men:

As you can see, the ad is for a gun. A "man card" identifies a person as being truly masculine, like a citizen's card (시민등록증/*simin deungnokjeung*) identifies someone as Korean or a foreign resident's card (외국인등록증/*oigukin deungnokjeung*) identifies someone as an international resident of Korea.

What image of masculinity does this ad give, if the gun is the correct answer, and the kitten or the candle is a wrong answer? What does this tell young men who might see the ad about appropriate masculine behavior?

Find the video of a 2007 PSA (Public Service Announcement) titled "Stop the bullets. Kill the gun."[9]

9) youtube.com/watch?v=ylvAovoO2kk

Discuss your experience of watching the video. Do you think it is an effective video? Explain. The music for the video is from "Casta Diva," the aria from Bellini's opera *Norma*. Discuss what the music adds to the experience of the video. Find out a little bit about the aria, especially its lyrics, in preparing for the discussion.

The PSA identified in the previous question has a watermelon in it. Watch these two videos and consider the watermelons in them. What is the connection to the PSA? The two videos: "Glock Shot Placement: Double-Tap to COM, Head-Shot Safety" (a Glock is a kind of handgun)[10] and "FN Five Seven Shooting."[11]

Jackson Katz (above) refers to a famous scene from the 1939 movie, *The Wizard of Oz*. Almost all Americans would understand what he means by the reference. Make an internet search for "The Wizard of Oz: Pay No Attention," and watch the video you find.[12] How does the video clip from the movie show Katz's point?

Jackson Katz also refers to the "Marlboro Man ethos." Who was the Marlboro Man?

---

10) youtube.com/watch?v=moi7c8iwfnc

11) youtube.com/watch?v=qPjfP4L-Hwc

12) youtube.com/watch?v=NZR64EF3OpA

Topic 12

Images of Gender Difference in American Popular Culture

The symbols below were circulating on Facebook not too long ago because of an ongoing debate about *gender* issues in the U.S., about deviations from what some people consider traditional sexuality. The simple male-female heterosexual gender binary has been drawn into question for a long time in the U.S. The acronym LGBTQIA reflects that questioning. According to the online *Urban Dictionary*, the acronym stands for "Lesbian, Gay, Bisexual, Transsexual, Queer, Intersex, Asexual," and it is an "inclusive term . . . for people with non-mainstream sexual orientation or gender identity."

LGBTQIA rights are an ongoing issue in American society and culture. During the second decade of the 21st Century, several legal actions granted various rights to the LGBTQIA community. In 2011, a new law granted them the right to serve openly in the military; before then, it had been illegal for an "out"[1] homosexual to serve in the military. In June 2015, the Supreme Court of the United States ruled that marriage between same-sex partners was a constitutional

1) To be "out" is to "come out of the closet." That means a person who is open about his or her homosexuality, someone who may have tried to hide their true nature but has stopped hiding it.

right. That is, the court supported "marriage equality" for gay and lesbian couples. During the debates about marriage equality, the following image of a pink equal sign on a red background represented support for those non-traditional marriages.

Variations of this symbol include a yellow equal sign on a dark blue background.

Q : How do you think this symbol refers to the Declaration of Independence? Recall these words: "We hold these truths to be self-evident, that all men are created equal, that they are endowed by their Creator with certain unalienable Rights, that among these are Life, Liberty, and the pursuit of Happiness."

The equal sign in the marriage equality symbol refers

to the idea that "all men [indeed, all *people*] are created ***equal.***" The pink color represents LGBTQIA people. As the Supreme Court recognized, "the pursuit of Happiness" should include the right to marry a person of one's own choosing, regardless of gender or sexual identity.

The legal changes to LGBTQIA rights were not supported by all Americans, however. During the debates about their rights on social media like Facebook, the following symbol began to appear, also pink on a red background. As you can see, the symbol responds to the marriage equality symbol by turning the lower horizontal line 90 degrees to a vertical position to create a cross.

Q : How do you think the symbol expresses opposition to LGBTQIA rights?

Many of you will recognize this as a symbol of

Christianity. Many conservative Christians accept the prohibitions against homosexuality expressed by some of the writers of the Bible. They also believe that the U.S. should be governed by Christian principles, even though freedom of religion is guaranteed in the Constitution.[2] Thus, this symbol indicates that the person using it believes that homosexual marriage should remain illegal because God has said it should be illegal. Not all Christians believe this. Many Christians support marriage equality with the belief that our understanding of the Bible should change as human knowledge about various topics becomes more complete.[3]

In this debate through symbols, the marriage equality supporters responded with yet another modification to the equal sign that referred again to American traditions and the Constitution:

2) The First Amendment to the Constitution includes this language: "Congress shall make no law respecting an establishment of religion, or prohibiting the free exercise thereof."

3) Another example of this difference is that some conservative Christians insist that God created the world in six days and reject scientific theories of evolution and the beginnings of the world. Other Christians believe that God led humans to science to help us better understand the world, and that this God-given knowledge helps us to understand the six-day creation story as a myth that people used when they understood very little about the cosmos.

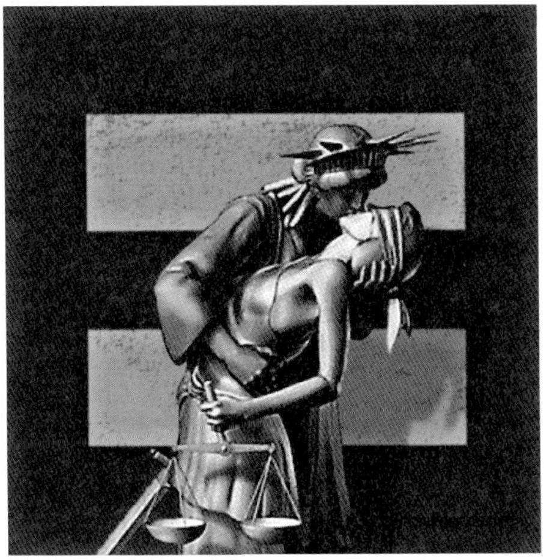

Q : Can you identify the two figures in this image?

You should notice that both of these figures are female. Probably everyone recognizes the figure with the points of light coming from her head. She is the Statue of Liberty who stands in New York Harbor, with the following inscription: "Give me your tired, your poor, your huddled masses yearning to breathe free, the wretched refuse of your teeming shore. Send these, the homeless, tempest-tossed to me, I lift my lamp beside the golden door!" The other figure is Lady Justice, who is represented by statues at courthouses throughout the world, including the U.S. Supreme Court building.[4)]

---

4) The image of Liberty kissing Justice was created by Mirko Ilic for an article by Laura Conaway titled "I'd Leave the Country, But My Wife Won't Let Me" (*Village Voice* 24 February 2004. Web.)

Lady Liberty, of course, recalls one of the "unalienable rights" asserted in the Declaration of Independence: "Life, *Liberty*, and the pursuit of Happiness." If you recall the Pledge of Allegiance discussed earlier (Chapter 6), you will see that the two ladies are included there as well: "I pledge allegiance to the flag of the United States of America, and to the republic for which it stands, one nation under God, indivisible, with *liberty and justice for all.*" The image of the two ladies also seems to want to remind people that these rights are "for all," even those who have a sexuality (or sexualities) that differ from the heterosexual majority. Indeed, much of American history has involved struggles to protect the rights of various minority populations.

Considering the occasional references to Korean Americans and other Asian Americans, we might ask, "What do Asian Americans think about LGBT rights?"

Q : Before reading further, what do you think is the answer to the question about Asian Americans, especially Korean Americans, and LGBTQ rights? Now, see how your answer matches the information below.

In an article that appeared on the website for *KoreAm: The Korean American Experience* (now changed to *Kore*) in 2013, "A Look at Same-Sex Marriage in the Korean American

Community," the author wrote:[5)]

> Even as the rest of the nation seems to be moving toward greater acceptance of same-sex marriage, polls show that Korean Americans chart some of the highest rates of opposition to it. With the U.S. Supreme Court possibly issuing a landmark ruling on same-sex marriage this month, *KoreAm* revisits the controversial topic, examining a community still clearly struggling with accepting LGBTQ-identified people among us—but also revealing glimmers of hope and change.

Another article from the same website reported that, in the words of the title, "Korean Americans Oppose Gay Marriage More Than Any Asian Group."[6)] The article reported on a study conducted by the National Asian American Survey. For all Asian Americans surveyed about whether or not they supported LGBT Marriage Rights, 12% said they "don't know"; 26% said they "strongly oppose"; 26% said they "oppose"; 24% said they "favor"; 11% said they "strongly favor." For Korean Americans, the numbers for the same question were 4% "don't know"; 51% "strongly oppose"; 22% "oppose"; 16% "support"; 6% "strongly favor." The full numbers are in the chart below. Korean Americans were the only group in which over half of the

5) 20 June 2013. kore.am/june-issue-a-look-at-same-sex-marriage-in-the-korean-american-community/

6) 2 May 2013. kore.am/korean-americans-oppose-gay-marriage-more-than-any-asian-group-survey-says/

respondents replied "strongly oppose."

	Don't Know	Strongly Oppose	Oppose	Favor	Strongly Favor
Korean	4	51	22	16	6
Cambodian	24	8	20	33	15
Chinese	11	30	19	30	11
Filipino	9	28	34	19	10
Hmong	14	19	21	40	6
Indian	13	12	33	26	17
Japanese	10	15	24	30	21
Vietnamese	30	17	32	19	3
TOTAL	12	26	27	24	11

FOR FURTHER CONSIDERATION

What are the attitudes toward homosexuality in your country?

Compare this photograph, which is famous in the U.S., with the image of Lady Liberty kissing Lady Justice. This was taken in 1945 in New York City at a celebration of the end of World War II. The young sailor grabbed a nurse and kissed her. For many years, this was seen as a picture that shows the people's joy about the end of the war.7) When

we understand that the woman in the photo did not give her permission for the kiss, there might be another way to understand the meaning of the photo.[8] To consider the way the "marriage equality" image slightly alters the photograph, compare Lady Liberty's hand supporting the back of Lady Justice's head with the way the sailor holds the nurse's head. You might also consider the nurses left hand with Lady Justice's left hand, which continues to hold the scales of justice in their proper position.

7) Maureen Callahan, "The True Story behind the Iconic V-J Day Sailor and 'Nurse' Smooch," *NY Post* 17 June 2012. nypost.com/2012/06/17/the-true-story-behind-the-iconic-v-j-day-sailor-and-nurse-smooch/

8) "The Kissing Sailor, or 'The Selective Blindness of Rape Culture'," *Crates and Ribbons: In Pursuit of Gender Equality* 30 September 2012. cratesandribbons.com/2012/09/30/the-kissing-sailor-or-the-selective-blindness-of-rape-culture-vj-day-times-square/

Topic 13

Holidays in America

Americans spend a lot of their leisure time playing or watching sports and other recreational activities, or watching media that relay ideas of gender to viewers. Holidays offer other leisure times for Americans. There are ten U.S.A. Federal Holidays — the days off for people who work for the federal government (the post office will be closed on these days, for instance); some other employees get some or all of these days off; almost everyone gets at least four of these days off (which four, do you think?); if a holiday falls on weekend, the day off will be on either the preceding Friday or the following Monday.

Here are the ten federal holidays and the dates for each of them.

January 1	Christmas Day
Third Monday in January	Columbus Day
Third Monday in February	Independence Day
Last Monday in May	Labor Day
July 4	Martin Luther King, Jr. Day
First Monday in September	Memorial Day
Second Monday in October	New Year's Day
November 11	Presidents' Day
Fourth Thursday in November	Thanksgiving Day
December 25	Veterans Day

Q : What does each of the holidays celebrate? Some are obvious; others perhaps not so obvious.

Q : See how many of the holidays on the right you can match with the dates on the left. (The answers are at the end of the chapter.)

Christmas is celebrated in various ways, including not at all. It is one of two federal holidays that has a direct connection to America's Christian heritage; the other is Thanksgiving. Some of the customs of celebrating Christmas are often observed even by non-Christians, and not observed by some denominations of Christianity, like Jehovah's Witnesses. These customs include giving and receiving gifts, decorating one's house and yard with Christmas lights and decorations, decorating a Christmas tree inside the house, and singing Christmas songs like "Rudolph, The Red-nosed Reindeer" and "Jingle Bells."[1] Many radio stations play Christmas music, beginning about a month before Christmas Day.

Many Christians also celebrate the holiday by going to church, especially on Christmas Eve (the night before Christmas), when many churches hold candlelight services and sing religious Christmas songs like "Silent Night" and "Joy to the World." Christians include many decorations

1) Easy to find on *Youtube.*

with Christian themes and imagery on their trees and in their yards. Christmas is, of course, a day named for Jesus Christ, and it is a remembrance of his birth. That is what Christians refer to as "the real meaning" of Christmas.

Several other holidays are celebrated around Christmastime as well. Hanukkah is a Jewish holiday that is celebrated for eight days and nights. Kwanzaa is a celebration of community developed by African Americans and based on African traditions. Because of that cluster of holidays and because New Year's Day is just a week after Christmas, people often greet one another with the phrase, "Happy Holidays." That phrase is controversial, as it makes some (certainly not all) Christians angry. Because Christmas is a Christian holiday, and, according to those Christians, the U.S. is a Christian nation, they insist people should say "Merry Christmas" to keep focus on "the real meaning of Christmas." If the U.S. president sends out cards that say "Happy Holidays" rather than "Merry Christmas," those Christians express loud public outrage. One year, they even protested Starbucks because their holiday cups did not reflect Christian beliefs. In 2015, CNN online reported, "This year's holiday season red cups at Starbucks have stirred up critics who accuse the company of waging a war on Christmas."[2)]

The other national holiday connected to the Christian tradition is Thanksgiving, which was first designated

2) Jackie Wattles, "Starbucks' Plain Red Holiday Cups Stir Up Controversy" 9 November 2015. money.cnn.com/2015/11/08/news/ companies/starbucks-red-cups-controversy/

as a national holiday by Abraham Lincoln in 1863. Thanksgiving commemorates the first harvest by the Pilgrim immigrants to America in 1621, when, according to legend, they celebrated with their Native American neighbors, without whom they would have starved in the winter of 1620. The religious nature of the holiday lies in the fact that the Pilgrims were a Christian group who came to America so they would be free to practice their own type of Christianity without government interference. Americans gather with family members to eat and watch football and Thanksgiving parades on television. The traditional main dish is roast turkey, often accompanied by mashed potatoes, candied yams, cranberry sauce, and pumpkin pie, among other food.

Thanksgiving is celebrated about a month before Christmas, and always on a Thursday. The day after Thanksgiving is **Black Friday**, which is not an official national holiday. Indeed, for the past few years, Black Friday has come to Korea. Black Friday is the semi-official beginning of the Christmas shopping season, and many stores offer deeply discounted products.

Q : Why do you think Black Friday is called "Black" Friday?

Independence Day is celebrated during the summer, and it is a celebration of the very idea of and the founding of America. It is held on the day that the Declaration of Independence was signed (see Chapter 4). U.S. Americans celebrate the day with parades, celebrations at local parks, cook-outs, and fireworks after the sun goes down. If you use an internet search engine and search for "fourth of july parade images," or replace "parade" with some other search term like "fireworks" or "celebration" or "picnic," you will get a good feel for the holiday.

Independence Day is a secular holiday; Christmas is a religious holiday; Thanksgiving is somewhere in between. However, religion, particularly Christianity, is a prominent element of secular as well as religious holidays in the U.S. Many Independence Day events include prayers offered by local Christian clergy, and clergy of other faiths like Judaism or Islam also participate in some places. The connection between religion and patriotism was noted earlier in the discussion of manifest destiny. We might consider Independence Day to reflect a kind of *civil religion*.

Q : What is civil religion, do you think? Is it a good or bad thing? A little of each? What aspect of civil religion might you find in your own country?

There are other special days that many people celebrate, although they are not official U.S. holidays.[3] Some are similar

3) Look here for a list of even more special days in the U.S.: www.timeanddate.com/holidays/us/

to *Pepero Day* in Korea (Korean students might want to explain to their classmates why *Pepero Day* is on November 11, as well as why Pepero are called Pepero). Some of these days, like Valentine's Day or Mother's Day, are remembered by almost everyone. Others, like National Donut Day, are unknown to most people. Some of these days, like April 15, people would like to forget. But they better not forget that one, or they will be in trouble with the IRS (Internal Revenue Service) and have to pay a penalty.

- Groundhog Day. February 2nd.
- St. Valentine's Day. February 14th.
- Fat Tuesday/Shrove Tuesday/Mardi Gras. The Tuesday before Lent begins.
- Ash Wednesday. The first day of Lent.
- St. Patrick's Day. March 17th.
- April Fools' Day. April 1st.
- Good Friday. The Friday before Easter Sunday.
- Easter Sunday. Usually in early to mid-April; sometimes in late March.
- Tax Day. April 15.
- Cinco de Mayo. May 5th.
- Mother's Day. 2nd Sunday in May.
- National Doughnut Day. 1st Friday of June.
- Flag Day. June 14th.
- Father's Day. 3rd Sunday in June.

- Parents' Day. 4th Sunday in July.
- Grandparents' Day. First Sunday after Labor Day.
- Halloween. Oct 31st.
- Black Friday. The Friday after Thanksgiving.
- Pearl Harbor Remembrance Day. December 7th.
- Hanukkah. Celebrated for eight days, usually in December.
- Kwanzaa. December 26th to January 1st.
- New Year's Eve. December 31st.

FOR FURTHER CONSIDERATION

Dates for U.S.A. Federal Holidays:

January 1	New Year's Day
Third Monday in January	Presidents' Day
Third Monday in February	Martin Luther King, Jr. Day
Last Monday in May	Memorial Day
July 4	Independence Day
First Monday in September	Labor Day
Second Monday in October	Columbus Day
November 11	Veterans Day
Fourth Thursday in November	Thanksgiving Day
December 25	Christmas Day

Columbus Day has become a very controversial holiday in the U.S. Find out what the day celebrates, what the controversy is about, and what that says about diversity as it was discussed in Chapter 1.

Clement Clarke Moore (1779 - 1863) wrote the poem "Twas the Night before Christmas" ("twas" is a contraction for "it was"), also called "A Visit from St. Nicholas," in 1822. It is now a tradition in many American families to read the poem during the Christmas season, often on Christmas Eve. Here is the first stanza of the poem.

> 'Twas the night before Christmas, when all through the house
> Not a creature was stirring, not even a mouse.
> The stockings were hung by the chimney with care,
> In hopes that St. Nicholas soon would be there.

Who is St. Nicholas? What name does he use these days? Find the poem online and consider if there is or is not any connection to "the real meaning of Christmas" in the poem. [4]

Explore the customs about one or a few of the special days that are not national holidays. Easter is the holiday in the photo below. The event below is not a religious event,

---

4) www.poetryfoundation.org/poems-and-poets/poems/detail/43171

but the day is a religious holiday.

The photograph depicts an "Easter egg hunt." The mythical Easter Bunny delivers baskets of candy, Easter eggs, and sometimes little toys to children. Sometimes the Easter Bunny leaves those things hidden outdoors or indoors, and the children have to search for them. Often, families will dye Easter eggs together. I used to do it every year with my mother and then every year with my children.

Americans like to eat chocolate Easter bunnies. Indeed, it seems that Americans like anything made of chocolate: about one-third of Americans are obese, which means to weigh so much that your health may be threatened. 4-5% of Koreans are obese. Korea seems to be catching up, however: about 65% of Americans and about 30% of Koreans are overweight.[5] The photo below includes two

5) www.oecd.org/health/obesity-update.htm

chocolate bunnies of the kind that are often found in Easter baskets. Someone has taken a bite out of each bunny.

If you would like to know more about holidays, here is a good U.S. Embassy resource:

infopedia.usembassy.or.kr/ENG/_f_1001.html

Topic 14

Music and Society—An Introduction

One of the most pervasive aspects of popular culture is popular music. We hear it almost everywhere. The U.S. has been the source of great creativity in music. It has given the world jazz, blues, bluegrass, country-western, rock and roll, and rap. Those styles have influenced music throughout the world. Recall that LeRoy Ashby wrote that "popular culture has become the nation's leading export" (see Chapter 2), and popular music is one of America's chief cultural exports. For instance, rap, which was first developed by African-Caribbean immigrants to New York in the 1970s, has taken on various styles and local variations from Africa to Asia, Kenya to South Korea.

Like many developments in American music such as jazz, blues, and rock, rap music has its roots in the African-American community. Today, however, it is popular with all ethnic groups. In its early days, rap often reflected a social consciousness that opposed the dominant culture. Sometimes, rappers still take that socially conscious stance. In that respect, it is like other kinds of music that have developed in the U.S. That oppositional connection between the 1970s and today reminds us of Carl Weinberg's claim that popular culture "offers a wealth of bridges between the past and present" (see Chapter 2).

For an example of such a bridge from past to present that does not obviously reflect an oppositional consciousness, consider two videos that are easily available online: Marilyn Monroe singing "Diamonds Are a Girl's Best Friend"[1] and Madonna singing "Material Girl."[2] "Diamonds Are a Girl's Best Friend" was originally written for a 1949 Broadway play called *Gentlemen Prefer Blondes*. Broadway musicals are a great source of music in American popular culture. That play was turned into a 1953 movie of the same title. That movie starred Marilyn Monroe, one of America's film-land "sex symbols."

After finding a video of the song online, you might consider how it communicates ideas of gender as discussed in Chapter 10. You can find all of the lyrics online, but this brief sample will suggest the main point of the song.

> Men grow cold
> As girls grow old,
> And we all lose our charms in the end.
>
> But square-cut or pear-shaped,
> These rocks don't lose their shape.
> Diamonds are a girl's best friend.

The main point of the song is that a young woman should trade her beauty for jewelry, especially diamonds,

1) vimeo.com/59843065
2) youtube.com/watch?v=DNSUOFgj97M

because diamonds are better and more faithful friends than men. Basically, diamonds and other valuables she gets from her male suitors are her retirement plan. She advises women to get as much as they can while they are young and attractive.

Q : Find all of the lyrics to "Diamonds Are a Girl's Best Friend" and see if you need help in understanding any of them.

In "Material Girl," a music video that came out in 1984, Madonna refers to the past and Marilyn Monroe's song. The most obvious reference is simply in the visual aspects of the song presentations. Madonna wears an exact copy of Marilyn Monroe's dress, and she dances with a group of men who wear almost exactly the same clothes as the men in Marilyn Monroe's movie performance.

At one point in "Diamonds Are a Girl's Best Friend," the male dancers circle around Monroe and flash jewels at her to get her attention. Madonna replicates that moment in her video.

The similarities are much more than just visual. Madonna sings about the same idea that Monroe sang about. Madonna's character rejects the boys who offer only romance

'cause the boy with the cold hard cash
Is always mister right, 'cause we are
Living in a material world,
And I am a material girl.

She is materialistic, which might be a negative aspect of the American emphases on success and individualism. Unlike the Monroe song, however, the music video tells a story that contradicts the message of the song. While the character in the music video sings a song in which she claims to like men for their money, when the singer is offstage, she actually rejects a man who tries to win her with diamonds. Apparently, she makes her own money and does not need a man to survive. Another man who wins her heart in the end at first wants to give her expensive gifts. He does not win her heart until he woos her with a simple small bouquet of flowers and gives her a ride in an old truck. It seems that simplicity and love are better than money.

Q : Find all of the lyrics to "Material Girl" and see if you need help in understanding any of them.

The connections between songs are not just across time but also across borders. Take the example of Han Dae Su (한대수), who grew up in Korea and New York City in the 1950s and 60s. While in New York, he absorbed many influences from the folk music scene. When he returned to Korea, he did his military service then published two albums. One of the songs on the first album, "*Mul Jom Juso*" (물좀주소 – Give Me Some Water),[3] represents transnational relationships in popular music, but it also demonstrates that popular music can also be part of counter culture. Much of the music Han absorbed in New York was opposed to the "American Dream" that imagined individuals attaining their economic and social goals with no regard for others in society. That music often opposed the political system that they saw as part of the "military-industrial complex."[4]

Han Dae Su's songs were received as counter culture and banned by the administration of Park Chung Hee. Han then returned to New York, but has since come back to Korea. In this song, he asks for water because, he says, his

3) youtube.com/watch?v=diyZpivceAg

4) A term given by President Dwight Eisenhower in the 1950s, who warned against allowing an alliance between America's military and its major industries that could come to control politics and society. Some today think that Eisenhower was prophetic and his fears have come true. Others would disagree.

throat is dry. This is a coded song. In the code, water represents something other than itself. At one point, he sings that water is love. A more counter-cultural reading might argue that the water and represent democracy, and the early seventies when the song came out (1971) were times of authoritarian oppression of democratic impulses in Korea. This is a protest song. He cannot say he wants democracy because he would be censored, even arrested, so he says "water" instead. In spite of the code, the song was banned.

Q : Try to translate the lyrics of "*Mul Jom Juso*" into English and explain them to any international students in the class.

As we see from these examples, popular culture can accept the way things are, as "Diamonds Are a Girl's Best Friend" seems to do with cultural conventions of femininity. On the other hand, popular culture can use those cultural conventions to subvert them, as "Material Girl" might do (and might not – both positions have some merit). Popular culture might also act as counter culture to challenge political power structures, as "*Mul Jom Juso*" does in its coded language. Whether or not an example of popular culture challenges convention, we should ask ourselves what it shows about our time and place, what it says about us and the way we live. We should consider how we can apply critical thinking skills toward contemporary popular culture to become better consumers, better citizens, and more aware human beings.

If we think of American popular music and its relationship to the past, it is clear that people have often challenged convention and political power in their music: sometimes one, sometimes the other, and sometimes both. In order to trace the relationship of popular music to culture and politics, we will go back to the 1950s and the origins of rock and roll, a kind of music that disturbed the *status quo* and has influenced most developments in popular music since.

FOR FURTHER CONSIDERATION

Consider the idea of "commodification" in "Diamonds Are a Girl's Best Friend." What other ideas from Chapter 10 might be used in a critical analysis of that song or of Madonna's "Material Girl"?

Earlier, I made a few comparisons between the two songs and videos above. There are many other comparisons that one might make. See how many other ways that Madonna's video gives homage to "Diamonds Are a Girl's Best Friend." You can see these two songs brought together in another film, which came out in 2001, *Moulin Rouge.* Nicole Kidman plays a cabaret singer. One of her songs is "Diamonds Are a Girl's Best Friend." In the middle of the song, she inserts the chorus from "Material Girl": "For we are living in a material world, / and I am a material girl."[5)]

The U.S. Embassy offers two descriptions of *American Popular Music*. One is *American Popular Music* by Larry Starr and Christopher Waterman.[6)] The other is an *Info-pedia USA* page on *Arts and Entertainment*, which is available in both English and Korean.[7)] Consider one of those and report in writing or in speaking on what you discover.

Look at the following videos and consider how they show that popular culture often connects the present to the past and that American popular culture is a significant export with transnational influence:

- Diane Ross and the Supremes, "Stop! In the Name of Love" (1965) and "You Keep Me Hangin' On" (1966).[8)]
- "We're Your Dreamgirls" from the movie *Dreamgirls* (2006).[9)]
- Wonder Girls, "Nobody" (2008).[10)]

---

5) youtube.com/watch?v=xsOVE7QR9VI
6) photos.state.gov/libraries/korea/49271/dwoa_120909/american_popular_music.pdf
7) infopedia.usembassy.or.kr/ENG/_f_0601.html
8) youtube.com/watch?v=JC-MDYopSoA&feature=related; youtube.com/watch?v=lxny2KMd0TI
9) youtube.com/watch?v=fbNz1vlRSyM

Finally, to see where Lady Gaga got her name and to make another connection of the present to the past in popular culture, see "Radio Ga Ga" by the group Queen.[11) "Ga-ga" was originally a term that referred to the way babies make sounds before they learn how to use actual words ("ga-ga, goo-goo") and, thus, to sounds that make no sense.

---

10) Original Korean version: youtube.com/watch?v=yz9LQy0rmq0. English version: youtube.com/watch?v=BA7fdSkp8ds

11) youtube.com/watch?v=azdwsXLmrHE

Topic 15

Music and Society – the 50s

Our study of music in American society continues by going back to the past because the 1950s and 60s were marked by the development of rock and roll, a significant American contribution that has influenced world music ever since. Like the previous chapter, this chapter helps build understanding of the connections between past and present in popular culture.

The 1950s are generally seen as a very conservative time in American culture and society. It was a prosperous time for many Americans. The U.S. had helped defeat Germany, Japan, and their allies in World War II in the 1940s and had become a major world power. While much of Europe and Asia had been scarred and damaged by the war, with homes, factories, and whole cities destroyed or crippled, the American infrastructure was preserved. No bombs had fallen on American cities, so American was able to prosper while other nations had to rebuild.

America presented a staunch anti-communist front, and many people who were considered to be too far to the left suffered under the anti-communist fervor led by Joseph McCarthy, a senator from Wisconsin. Just the accusation of being a communist could cost a person their job. A manifestation of this anti-communism was American involvement on the Korean peninsula before, during, and after the Korean War that lasted from 1950 to 1953. During this decade, the words "under God" were added to the Pledge of Allegiance (see Chapter 6), and the words "In God We Trust" were required by law to appear on all American money. Those government-imposed references to religious belief were intended as a defense against communistic thinking.

The 50s were a time that encouraged women to stay at home and men to go out and be the "breadwinners." Women were encouraged to support and obey their husbands. A famous (or infamous) article from a 1955 issue of *Housekeeping Monthly* called "The Good Wife's Guide" features an image of a woman greeting her husband as he comes home from work. She wears a dress, an apron, and high heels as she stands over the stove preparing dinner. Two nicely-dressed and clean young children greet their father. The house appears to be spotless, at least from the shiny floors. Of course, the wife has a big smile on her face. Women are advised to become "The Good Wife" in various ways: "Have dinner ready"; "Prepare yourself"; "Prepare the children"; "Make him comfortable"; "Don't complain if he's late home for dinner or even if he stays out all night"; and other means of subordinating themselves to their husbands.[1)]

---

1) To see an image of the article and read the complete list of advice, you can go to "How to Be a Good Wife in the 1950s" on the V*intage*

You should consider that many housewives of the time had worked throughout the Second World War. Many men were off fighting, so the women had to work in the factories and in all sorts of other jobs to keep the country running during the war. For some women it may have been difficult to subdue all of their desires in order to please their husbands.

During the 1950s, the American Dream seemed very possible for very many people. At least for many white male people. Black Americans still struggled for equality in education and opportunity. Nonetheless, some progress toward equality was made. The Korean War was the first American war in which black soldiers were permitted to serve in the same units with white soldiers. In 1954, the U.S. Supreme Court decided in "Brown vs. the Board of Education of Topeka, Kansas" that it was unconstitutional for states to establish separate schools for black and white students. That court case led to desegregation of public schools, although that desegregation was not fully implemented until the next decade.

Music also showed some cracks in the conservative, white-male dominated social structure. One big challenge to conservative convention was the advent of rock and roll. Rock and roll was created from two different streams of music. Bringing those two streams together recalls the racial integration of the military and the schools. One stream was so-called "race music"; that is music the came from the

---

Everyday website (posted September 6, 2016) at www.vintag.es/2016/09/how-to-be-good-wife-in-1950s.html.

African American community, primarily blues and jazz. The other stream was so-called "hillbilly music"; that is music that developed in rural white communities in America, and it is also known as country or country-western music. Rural communities are known as the "country," which is often opposed to the city.

An example from country music suggests how the conservative, often sexist, surface of 1950s culture was challenged by dissenting voices. In 1952, Hank Thompson came out with a country song titled "The Wild Side of Life."[2] Thompson sings of a man who loves a woman purely and deeply, but she keeps going out to meet other men at "honky-tonks." The *Google* dictionary defines a honky-tonk as "a cheap or disreputable bar, club, or dance hall, typically where country music is played." The refrain to the song goes like this:

> I didn't know God made honky-tonk angels.
> I might have known you'd never make a wife.
> You gave up the only one that ever loved you
> And went back to the wild side of life.

As you can see, this song, like the article from *Housekeeping Monthly*, attempts to enforce a conservative vision of appropriate femininity in the context of a Christian belief system. The reference to God suggests that the Christian deity is fundamental to this world view. Calling the woman

2) youtube.com/watch?v=Q5y5jWv2xQw.

an "angel" is ironic, since her fondness for "the wild side of life" is sinful rather than angelic. The message is that good women should stay home and not run out to bars without their husbands.

Q : Find all of the lyrics to "The Wild Side of Life" and see if you need help in understanding any of them.

There is no serious challenge to conservative cultural influences in that song, but Thompson's song was quickly challenged in the same year by Kitty Wells with her release of another country song, "It Wasn't God Who Made Honky-Tonk Angels."[3] As you can see by the title, Kitty Wells disagrees with Hank Thompson about the creation of honky-tonk angels. While Thompson blames women, Kitty Wells shifts the blame back to men.

Here is what Wells says about the creation of honky-tonk angels:

It wasn't God who made Honky-Tonk angels,
As you said in the words of your song.
Too many times married men think they're still single;
That has caused many a good girl to go wrong.

It's a shame that all the blame is on us women.

3) youtube.com/watch?v=tKleTa94dC8

It's not true that only you men feel the same.
From the start most every heart that's ever broken
Was because there always was a man to blame.

Kitty Wells clearly expects men to take their share of the blame. Those "married men" who "think they're still single" are chasing after other women as if they were not married, as if they were "still single." Wells is going to put the responsibility where it belongs, and "there always was a man to blame." Wells seems to protest against the sexism that was prevalent in the conservative 50s.

Q : Find all of the lyrics to "It Wasn't God Who Made Honky-Tonk Angels" and see if you need help in understanding any of them.

As noted, another key influence on rock and roll was the blues. The blues also refers to a feeling of sadness and depression, as in "I have the blues" or "I am feeling blue." That sadness (a Korean might call it *han* [한]) is at the heart of the blues, which has been defined as a kind of music that is "laughing to keep from crying." You can see the laughter that is based on tears and hardship in Willie Dixon's "Built for Comfort."[4] Probably the most famous recording of the song was by Howlin' Wolf, whose real name was Chester Burnett.

4) This song is from the early 60s not the 50s, but it is an interesting and amusing example of the blues. youtube.com/watch?v= M-qtmZHofMc

The humor occurs at the beginning of the song when the singer says that he does not want to be called "fat" in spite of his large size:

> Some folk built like this, some folk built like that,
> But the way I'm built, don't you call me fat
> Because I'm built for comfort, I ain't built for speed,
> But I got everything all the good girls need.

Like the title says, he is "built for comfort." Apparently, his large size makes him soft and comfortable for the hugging. Of course, big men like the singer cannot run fast because they "ain't built for speed." However, when the next line tells us that he has "everything all the good girls need," the idea of "speed" takes on a new and somewhat racy meaning. It is a kind of *double entendre*, which the *Google* online dictionary defines as "a word or phrase open to two interpretations, one of which is usually risqué or indecent." The innuendo of the last line suggests he is not a fast lover. He takes his time at love, and that is what the good girls need.

The fun continues in the song, but at one place, we can see that the fun also reflects the difficulties of being black in America. He sings, "I ain't got no diamonds, and I ain't got no gold." His lack of wealth indicates the state of African America in having paths to wealth and economic success blocked by racism. On the other hand, he does "have love to satisfy your soul." According to the singer, a satisfied soul is better than wealth. Perhaps that is true.

Q : Find all of the lyrics to "Built for Comfort" and see if you need help in understanding any of them.

As is suggested by the satisfying lack of "speed" in "Built for Comfort," some blues can be sexually suggestive. When the blues met hillbilly music and started to become rock and roll, the raciness of the blues sometimes changed. That raciness had to be cleaned up a bit for the music to become acceptable for radio play in most of conservative white America. With that in mind, it is interesting to compare two versions of the song "Hound Dog," one by the African American blues singer Big Mamma Thornton, released in 1953, and one by the most popular early rock and roller Elvis Presley, released in 1956.[5] Elvis become so popular that he was called "The King" – the king of rock and roll, that is. Year later, Michael Jackson, who was married for a while to Elvis's daughter Lisa Marie Presley, became known as "The King of Pop." Lisa Marie was fine royalty, with one king for a father and another for a husband.

Both versions of the song begin with the accusation that "You ain't nothing but a hound dog." When a person is called a hound dog, it is not a compliment. To call someone

5) Big Mamma: youtube.com/watch?v=JvbSXVc451Q. Elvis: youtube.com/watch?v=URayWTkEPYM.

a hound dog is to insult them. Elvis's hound dog is "crying all the time." He makes a lot of noise, but he never seems to do anything worth doing: "you ain't never caught a rabbit," sings Elvis. A hound dog is supposed to catch rabbits. So, if this hound dog cannot catch a rabbit, he is no good. He is someone who makes a big sound, maybe like bragging, but doesn't do anything to brag about. He might also be someone who complains a lot, since complaining is often called "crying." Elvis had heard that this hound dog was "high classed"; that is what "they said." However, "that was just a lie."

Big Mamma Thornton's hound dog is "high class," not according to someone else, but according to the hound dog himself. Like Elvis, Big Mamma sees that claim as a lie. Elvis's whitewashed version paints the hound dog as incompetent, a man of no ability. In that criticism of the hound dog, Elvis incorporates no obvious *double entendre.* The Big Mamma Thornton version, on the other hand, has some pretty racy *double entendre.* When she sings, "I ain't gonna [going to] feed you no more," she probably is not referring to actual food but to making love. You might recall the earlier discussion of how a woman might "Be Delicious" (Chapter 10). While an actual dog might come around for food to eat, the man who is a hound dog might be looking for the food of physical love.

While Elvis sang a much tamer version for mainstream radio audiences, he did help bring "race music" into the mainstream. Even though his "Hound Dog" is cleaned up from Thornton's version, he and his music were still seen as challenging the conservative *status quo*. Television was still a new thing in the 1950s, and when Elvis first appeared on the television, he was shown only above the waist because the way he shook his hips (see the video of "Hound Dog" for an example) was considered too sexually suggestive for television and family audiences. Today, the censorship of Elvis's hips might seem ridiculous.

Underneath the surface of the conservative façade of America society in the 50s, music showed some rebellion against the mainstream. Sometimes popular culture follows mainstream values, and sometimes it opposes them. Sometimes the oppositional voices become or are adapted to the mainstream. We can see that in many ways today. Be alert to the conjunctions of the mainstream and its oppositions in your own time.

FOR FURTHER CONSIDERATION

Find the "The Good Wife's Guide" mentioned above and read the list of a good wife's qualities and behaviors. As you read the list, consider parts of the advice that tell women they are lesser than or not as important as their husband, parts that tell readers that men are better than women. This, of course, is another image of women (see Chapter 10) that often occurs in the media, although not as often as it used to appear.

See if you can find more instances of possible double entendre in Big Mama Thornton's "Hound Dog." Some may be much more colorful than the one I noted above.

You might compare some of today's more risqué k-pop videos, or some of Nicki Minaj's videos ("Anaconda," for instance), with Elvis's relatively mild dance moves to think about how the world has changed.

Here is an image from 1943 that encouraged women to help in the effort to win World War II by working in factories while many young men were away at war. How does this image compare to the one give in "The Good Wife's Guide"? How does it differ from some of the images in Chapter 10 or other places in this book?

An instance of rebellion against strict conservative values of the 50s might be seen in the video for Elvis Presley's 1957 "Jailhouse Rock," taken from a movie of the same name and starring Presley.[6] As you watch the video, you can see that the short bit of narrative and the

6) youtube.com/watch?v=qka6JrKUM5U

costumes make this a forerunner of contemporary music videos. You could consider how Lady Gaga's 2009 video with Beyoncé, "Telephone," might allude to "Jailhouse Rock." If you think of the jailhouse as a metaphor for the strict confines of 50s culture and society, you might think of the energetic dance that breaks out in the jail as an attempt at freedom within the jailhouse of American society.

Topic 16

Music and Society – the 60s

The 60s were a time of turmoil, upheaval, and rebellion. The anti-communist feelings of the 50s continued into the 60s, and the military expression of those feelings shifted from East Asia to Southeast Asia with the American war in Vietnam. American involvement in Vietnam had begun as early as 1950, but a major military presence with large numbers of troops did not begin until the mid-60s. By the end of the 60s, more than half a million American troops were in Vietnam. As most people realize, South Korea was an ally of the U.S. in that war. As an aside, the South Korean film 님은 먼곳에 (*Nimeun Meon Gose*, 2008; titled *Sunny* when it appeared with English subtitles), is an interesting depiction of both Korean involvement in the Vietnam War and the influence of American rock and roll on Korean musical taste.

Another incidence of American anti-communism was the 1962 Cuban Missile Crisis. The Soviet Union (present-day Russia and the countries surrounding it) sent nuclear weapons to Cuba, which is less than 100 miles from the U.S. President John F. Kennedy surrounded Cuba with a naval blockade to prevent Russia from bringing in more missiles, and the U.S. demanded that the Soviet Union remove the ballistic missiles that had already been placed in Cuba. The blockade continued for 13 days in October, and the world seemed on the brink of nuclear war until the Soviet Union backed down and removed the missiles in exchange for a U.S. promise never to invade Cuba.

The Cuban missile crisis helped build an anti-war movement in the U.S., and that movement became so strong by the end of the 60s that thousands of university students demonstrated against the war throughout the U.S. The cracks in the conservative surface of the 50s that were revealed by the advent of rock and roll exploded into massive civil disobedience by various kinds of counter-cultural movements. One was the anti-war movement, another was the Civil Rights movement that continued to press demands for equal rights for black and brown people. The women's movement also found its own strong voice in the 60s.

The Civil Rights movement may be best known for its non-violent protests led by Dr. Martin Luther King, Jr. Some of the key events were the 1963 action in Birmingham, Alabama to force the city to desegregate public facilities. If you have ever seen any video of white police attacking young black people with dogs and fire hoses, those probably are from this action. Later in 1963, King and other Civil Rights leaders led the March on Washington at which he gave his famous "I Have a Dream" speech.[1] In 1965, King

1) Search for "Birmingham 1963" on *Youtube* to find many videos of the protests and the violent suppression of them by the police. The text of the "I Have a Dream" speech is available online at *The Martin Luther King, Jr. Research and Education Institute* of Stanford University. Videos of it are easy to find on the internet.

and other Civil Rights leaders organized a March from Selma, Alabama to the state capitol in Montgomery. On their first attempt, they were met by white police at the Edmund Pettus Bridge in Selma. The police violently attacked the marchers and the march was prevented. Finally, on the third try, with protection ordered by the President of the United States, the march was allowed to proceed. Those events have been dramatized in the 2014 film titled *Selma*.

The Civil Rights movement showed the power of popular culture through the still relatively new medium of television. As Americans throughout the country watched police terrorize non-violent black protestors on the evening news, there was growing support for ensuring equal rights for black people by passing laws. The two most important congressional acts were the Civil Rights Act of 1964 and the Voting Rights Act of 1965.

Sometimes, African American protests turned violent, and there were riots in city streets. Some of the more famous disturbances were in Watts, a predominantly black Los Angeles neighborhood, in 1965, Detroit in 1967, and throughout the country after the murder of Martin Luther King, Jr. in 1968.

That murder reflects one aspect of the social turmoil that marked the 1960s. John F Kennedy, the President of the United States, was assassinated on November 22, 1963. Malcolm X, an influential Black Muslim Civil Rights leader, was assassinated on February 21, 1965. King was assassinated on April 4, 1968. Just two months later, Robert Kennedy, the younger brother of John, was assassinated on June 6. Two of these deaths were eulogized by the singer Dion in 1968 with his song "Abraham, Martin, and John."[2] Abraham was Abraham Lincoln, the president who was assassinated in 1865 after leading the U.S. through its Civil War. The other two men are King and the elder Kennedy. Later in 1968, "Bobby" (the nickname for Robert) was added to the song to commemorate the younger Kennedy.

Here is the first verse of the song, which is repeated with variation for each of the other characters who are eulogized.

> Anybody here seen my old friend Abraham?
> Can you tell me where he's gone?
> He freed a lot of people but it seems the good they die young;
> You know I just looked around and he's gone.

Q : Find all of the lyrics to "Abraham, Martin, and John" and see if you need help in understanding any of them.

Other songs of the sixties reflect the times as well. One of the most famous recording studies of the 1960s was Motown in Detroit (where a 1967 race riot took place). "Motown" is a reference to Detroit. Detroit was the

---

2) youtube.com/watch?v=ZBiH5fsKJB8

automobile manufacturing center of the U.S.; most of the major auto companies had factories in Detroit. Automobiles are powered by motors, so Detroit became known as the motor city. A synonym for "city" is "town"; "mo" is an abbreviation for "motor." Thus, Motown.

Motown records produced mostly African American recordings of a variety of popular music known as "soul," a word that refers to the spiritual essence some people claim for black people. Black men were sometimes referred to as "Soul Brothers," for instance. Several Motown groups were girl groups.

One of those female groups was Martha and the Vandellas, whose 1964 song "Dancing in the Streets" celebrated the joy of being a young person on a summer evening: "Summer's here and the time is right / For dancing in the streets."[3] Later in the song, the group tells listeners, "So come on, every guy grab a girl / Everywhere around the world." It sounds like everyone is encouraged to enjoy themselves by dancing to "a brand new beat." That is the most obvious level of understanding the song, but "dancing in the streets" is also understood as getting out and demonstrating for Civil Rights. The metaphor of "dancing" is an homage to the freedom movements that gave us a new and different world, "a brand new beat."

---

3) youtube.com/watch?v=CdvITn5cAVc

Q : Find all of the lyrics to "Dancing in the Streets" and see if you need help in understanding any of them.

Another even more famous Motown women's ensemble was Diana Ross and the Supremes, who sang songs like "Stop in the Name of Love" (1965) and "You Keep Me Hanging On" (1967), which you were asked to listen to in the "Further Consideration" for Chapter 14. This group sang few songs that can be given a counter-cultural interpretation, but they were very influential.

The 60s in America saw an increased interest in the women's movement. A song from the 60s became a symbol of that fight for equal rights across gender lines: "Respect," sung by Aretha Franklin in 1965.[4)] In that song, she calls for "R-E-S-P-E-C-T" from her man. That song helped make Franklin such a well-known star that most Americans know her simply as "Aretha." If you have any American friends, ask them if they know the singer named "Aretha." I think that most of them will identify Aretha Franklin.

Q : Find all of the lyrics to "Respect" and see if you need help in understanding any of them.

Anti-war protests against the Vietnam War rocked many college campuses in the second half of the 60s, but protests

4) youtube.com/watch?v=fzPXozDgvYs

against America's military-industrial complex started before then. Bob Dylan, who won the 2016 Nobel Prize for Literature, helped inspire the Peace Movement in the angry "Masters of War"[5] and the contemplative "Blowin' in the Wind"[6] from 1963 as well as the ironic "With God on Our Side" from 1964, which was discussed above as a reaction to the idea of manifest destiny.

> Dylan calls out to those master of war:
> You that build the big guns
> You that build the death planes
> You that build all the bombs
> You that hide behind walls
> You that hide behind desks

He recites their sins, insisting that even Jesus would not forgive them. He sings, "All the money you made / Will never buy back your soul." In the last verse of the song, he expresses this wish: "I hope that you die / And your death'll come soon."

In "Blowin' in the Wind," he asks, "How many times must the cannon balls fly / Before they're forever banned?" He finishes the song with a last question, "How many deaths will it take 'til he knows / That too many people have died?" The answer to both questions is "blowin' in the wind."

---

5) youtube.com/watch?v=exm7FN-t3PY

6) youtube.com/watch?v=vWwgrjjIMXA

Q : Find all of the lyrics to “Masters of War” and “Blowin’ in the Wind” to see if you need help in understanding any of them.

The yearning for peace was a major inspiration behind the “hippy” movement of the 60s. So-called hippies were young people who “dropped out” of society, refusing to join the world of everyday, boring work. A motto attributed to the hippies as well as the anti-war movement was “make love, not war.” 1967 was called “The Summer of Love,” and it is represented by young people moving to San Francisco, the main location of the hippy movement. A famous song that captures the spirit of that movement is Scott McKenzie’s “If You’re Going to San Francisco.”[7]

McKenzie had some advice for anyone going to that city: “be sure and wear some flowers in your hair.” Indeed, hippies were often called “flower people,” and the expression “flower power” was common as a way of advocating peace. It was not unusual to see cars painted over with flowers.

McKenzie told listeners that they would “meet some gentle people there” in San Francisco. Those people represented “a whole generation with a new explanation.” And he promised that “summertime would be a love-in there.”

Q : Find all of the lyrics to “If You’re Going to San Francisco” and see if you need help in

7) youtube.com/watch?v=7I0vkKy504U

understanding any of them.

That lovely desire for everyone to love one another was troubled the next year when, following Bobby Kennedy's assassination, Chicago was the scene of riots between protestors and police at the Democratic Convention to nominate the next Democratic presidential candidate. That candidate, Hubert Humphrey, lost the election to the Republican Richard Nixon that November. Nixon later was forced to resign for condoning criminal activity.

You might note that the word "hippy" shares a root with the words "hip" (to be up-to-date, aware of the most modern fashions in music and culture), "hip-hop," and "hipster."

The last gasp of the peace-loving and tumultuous 60s came on 1969 at the iconic Woodstock Rock Festival in New York. Many famous rock musicians played there. A band named Country Joe and the Fish played their anti-war anthem, "Feel Like I'm Fixin' to Die," which included the lines

> One, two, three, four,
> What are we fighting for?
> Don't ask me, I don't give a damn.
> Next stop is Vietnam.[8)]

8) youtube.com/watch?v=dATyZBEeDJ4

Q : Find all of the lyrics to "Feel Like I'm Fixin' to Die" and see if you need help in understanding any of them.

There was a conservative backlash against the counter-cultural movements of the 60s because some people considered those movements to be unpatriotic. "Love it or leave it" (it = U.S.A.) became a saying that expressed a dislike for the anti-war movement. That conservative movement, identified as "the silent majority," helped elect Richard Nixon. You can see that backlash in music. One of the most famous conservative anthems was Merle Haggard's "Okie from Muskogee," which appeared in 1969, the same year as Woodstock.[9)]

In this verse, you can see that Merle Haggard may have been thinking about Scott McKenzie's song:

We don't make a party out of lovin';
We like holdin' hands and pitchin' woo;
We don't let our hair grow long and shaggy,
Like the hippies out in San Francisco do.

No "love-in" for Merle Haggard. He prefers more innocent interactions between men and women, like hand holding. He uses a phrase for courting that was outdated even in 1969: "pitching woo." In looking at the rest of the lyrics to this song, consider ways in which it gives a patriotic

9) youtube.com/watch?v=68cbjlLFl4U

alternative to the counter cultural movements. Here are a few idiomatic phrases you need to know to understand the song:

> to burn a draft card: the draft refers to the government forcing some young men to join the military (to fight in Vietnam); every young man had a draft card with a number on it, and the government would draft people by those numbers; some young men burned their draft cards as a protest against the Vietnam War
>
> white lightning: powerful alcohol made by ordinary people not a licensed distillery
>
> Old Glory: the flag of the U.S.A.

Q : Find all of the lyrics to "Okie From Muskogee" and see if you need help in understanding any of them.

FOR FURTHER CONSIDERATION

Report on the history of one or both of these record companies: Motown Records and Sun Records.

Compare the metaphors of dancing in "Dancing in the Streets" and "Jailhouse Rock" as they might reflect a desire for different kinds of freedom.

Compare Aretha's sentiments in "Respect" with Kitty Wells' sentiments in "It Wasn't God Who Made Honky-Tonk Angels." How are the attitudes similar? How do they differ?

"Stop in the Name of Love" and "You Keep Me Hanging On" by Diana Ross and the Supremes put women in a subordinate position in relation to men, unlike Aretha's "Respect." Discuss the ways in which the Supremes' songs show that subordination.

Bob Dylan, a songwriter, was awarded the Nobel Prize for Literature in 2016. Some people applauded the selection; other people argued that popular songs are not literature and that selecting Dylan diminished the award. Read a little bit about the controversy, and give your own opinion.

If you can find a copy, watch the South Korean film 님은 먼곳에 (*Nimeun Meon Gose*, 2008; titled *Sunny* when it appeared with English subtitles) or 고고70 (*Go-Go* Chilship, 2008; *Go-Go 70s* in English) and discuss the importance of American popular music in each.

Topic 17

Music and Society — the 70s, 80s, and 90s to the Present

The Vietnam War ended in the early 70s, with all American troops leaving the country by 1973. The U.S. loss in the war contributed to what was called American "malaise," a word used to describe the perception of Jimmy Carter, who was the president of the U.S. at that time (1977-81). The word has been defined as a "general feeling of not being healthy or happy." Besides losing a war to a small Southeast Asian country, the U.S. saw a president resign in disgrace (Richard Nixon in 1974), two oil crises (1973 and 1979) that limited supplies and increased prices, an Iranian revolution in which 53 American were held hostage for 444 days, and rising inflation and unemployment.

Popular music responded to that time of malaise in various ways. Bruce Springsteen produced rock songs like "Thunder Road"[1)] and "Born to Run"[2)] (1975) that expressed blue-collar (working class) frustrations. Both of those songs reflect a desire to escape from a place that offers little hope for a better future. They seem to ask the question, "Is the

1) www.youtube.com/watch?v=JGBXnw86Mgc, www.youtube.com/watch?v=x5kXnq5IjdU

2) www.youtube.com/watch?v=f3t9SfrfDZM, www.youtube.com/watch?v=IxuThNgl3YA

American Dream dead?"

Q : Find the lyrics to "Thunder Road" and "Born to Run" and see if you need help in understanding any of them.

The 1970s brought disco music which was composed for dancing. A 1977 movie, *Saturday Night Fever*, became iconic for its representation of the disco life.[3] It stars John Travolta as a working-class hero who lives only to dance—that is his "Saturday night fever." He has few social concerns and just wants to escape into the music.

The theme song for the movie was "Stayin' Alive" by the Bee Gees.[4] The band was British, but the movie is very American in its themes and settings. Part of the refrain from the song is "Life goin' nowhere, somebody help me." The main character in the film has a life that is "going nowhere." He seems to have no hope. Like the other people mentioned in the song, he is just "staying alive."

Q : Find the lyrics to "Stayin' Alive" and see if you need help in understanding any of them.

The frustrations with American life surface in a new

---

3) Learn more about the movie by going to IMDB (Internet Movie Database) or watching the trailer. IMDB: www.imdb.com/title/ tt0076666/;the trailer: www.youtube.com/watch?v=u1qN6gLbUMw

4) www.youtube.com/watch?v=_Vj092UgKwQ

stream of rock music, "New Wave." A representative group in the new wave was the Talking Heads. The band's name comes from the people on television, like news announcers and politicians, since we see just their heads on the screen, and those heads are just talking, telling us what to know and how to think.

The Talking Heads became famous in the 70s, but one of their biggest hits came out on 1983, two years after Ronald Reagan became president (1981-89) in a conservative revival that lasted throughout the 80s. "Burning Down the House" resisted this revival.[5] You could find the lyrics and explore them for how they reflect a frustration with regular middle-class life, how they question the American dream. You can also consider how you might dance to the music.

Q : Find the lyrics to "Burning Down the House" and see if you need help in understanding any of them.

The 1980s continued the high unemployment of the 70s and showed a growing gap between the wealthy and the poor and middle classes, a gap that has continued to widen into the present. On the other hand, popular culture experienced some great innovations in music. For instance, the Walkman hit the markets in 1980. The Walkman was a portable cassette player with headphones.

5) www.youtube.com/watch?v=xNnAvTTaJjM

People were now able to take their favorite music anywhere and listen to it. Today, this may not sound very impressive, but you must consider a world in which a small portable music player had never before existed.

Another 1980s technological innovation that represents world-changing events was the introduction of the Apple Macintosh in 1984. While it was not the first personal computer, it was the first one with a mouse. Personal computers did not yet have enough memory to play music, and there was no internet for most people yet, but the wide availability of personal computers helped change the way we work, learn, and play.

MTV (Music TV) began broadcasting in 1981, so people could turn on the television almost any time to watch popular music videos. Ever since then, the music video has been a major means of presenting popular music, although now more people watch those videos on the internet than on broadcast television, and they often watch them on their smart phones. One of the music videos that came to represent the power of combining music and images via MTV was Michael Jackson's "Thriller" (1983).[6] That video used the American b-movie tradition of horror films, including a voice-over by Vincent Price, who had become one of the iconic voices of those movies in the 1960s. In this video, Jackson, the "King of Pop," used the conventions of the zombie film, a genre that has again become popular in the second decade of the 21st-century.

Q : Find the lyrics to "Thriller" and see if you need help in understanding any of them.

Along with MTV, the greatest innovation in popular music of the 80s was rap. This form of music came out of hip-hop, a development that began at neighborhood "block parties" of the African American community in the Bronx in New York City. Hip-hop consists of at least four parts. One is rap music or MCing. The others are break dancing, graffiti, and DJing. Hip-hop culture actually originated in the 70s, and the first recording to gain mainstream popularity was Sugarhill Gang's "Rapper's Delight" in 1979. The music and culture gained widespread national and international popularity in the 80s. These days, many rap recordings emphasize the rapper's wealth and sexual prowess. Sometimes, they glorify violence, but the first rap song to gain popularity

6) Long version: www.youtube.com/watch?v=sOnqjkJTMaA Shorter version: www.youtube.com/watch?v=4V90AmXnguw

through MTV, like many other rap songs, reflects the "grassroots" origins of hip-hop.

That song is "The Message" by Grandmaster Flash and the Furious Five from 1982.[7] The group represents the ordinary people of the inner city, as you can see from their varied dress and the setting of the music video. They struggle in a world with very little opportunity to succeed. This song represents a kind of "counterculture" that is opposed to social, political, and economic systems that oppress minority groups, especially blacks, in the U.S. The refrain to the song indicates the frustration of growing up in a place without opportunity, a place where many young people turn to crime as a means of survival: "It's like a jungle sometimes. / It makes me wonder how I keep from goin' under." The inner city, with its poverty and crime, is the "jungle," where the strong survive and the weak get destroyed. It is hard not to "go under"; that is a metaphor of drowning, and the sea in which the singer drowns is the world that gives little opportunity to escape poverty. When someone tries to escape, some obstacle always stands in the way. The song tries to advise young people to stay in school because the attraction of money and power in crime too often leads to jail and an early death.

Q : Find the lyrics to "The Message" and see if you need help in understanding any of them.

Often, rap music is party music, and it has been from

7) www.youtube.com/watch?v=O4o8TeqKhgY

the beginning. People need some relief from the everyday world, and party music can help in that. But rap also often shows the social conscience that we hear in "The Message."

In 1987, Public Enemy came out with "Fight the Power ."[8] This song is a protest against the white-dominated power structure. It is also a poem with a message about freedom and equality for black people. It was made famous as a featured song in Spike Lee's 1989 film "Do the Right Thing,"[9] which reflected tensions between black men and the police and between blacks and Korean grocers.

Q : Find the lyrics to "Fight the Power" and see if you need help in understanding any of them.

In 1988, NWA released "Straight Outta Compton."[10] This song, along with others ("Fuck the Police") from the album of the same name, also represents a counterculture that is opposed to the dominant power structure. Rather than social and community awareness, however, this song expresses a masculinity that emphasizes violence and sexual power over women.[11] This is an example of "gangsta" rap, with images of sex and violence. According to Tricia Rose, the major scholar of hip-hop,[12] this sort of rap has become

8) www.youtube.com/watch?v=8PaoLy7PHwk

9) www.youtube.com/watch?v=muc7xqdHudI

10) www.youtube.com/watch?v=TMZi25Pq3T8

11) The 2015 film "Straight Outta Compton" tells the story of how NWA got together and broke apart.

most dominant because the small recording companies that helped popularize rap were sold to larger media companies, and those companies have promoted sex and violence above socially conscious music. She sees this as a kind of racism that elevates negative images of black people as "thugs." The recording companies claim this is what people want; Rose claims that the record companies have created the audience by promoting this "gangsta" rap over socially conscious music.

Q : Find the lyrics to "Straight Outta Compton" and see if you need help in understanding any of them.

The differences between the haves (people with wealth and opportunity) and the have-nots (people without much wealth or opportunity) continued throughout the 90s. At least one innovation would eventually give everyone greater access to information, as well as misinformation: the World Wide Web was begun in 1992. It would be a while before people could stream music over the internet or before sophisticated graphics were possible, but this innovation made all that possible.

Rap music continued as a major musical force in the 90s, and Public Enemy released "Can't Truss It" in 1991

12) *Black Noise: Rap Music and Black Culture in Contemporary America.* Middletown, CT: Wesleyan UP, 1994.
The Hip Hop Wars: What We Talk About When We Talk About Hip Hop—and Why It Matters. NY: Basic Books, 2008.

(truss = trust).[13] This song and video is a sophisticated combination of words and images building two parallel stories, one from the past during the days of slavery, and one from the present. *Genius.com* quotes a 1991 interview in which Chuck D, a member of Public Enemy, describes the meaning of the song and video like this:

> "Can't Truss It" is about how the corporate world of today is just a different kind of slavery. We don't control what we create. And because of the media, we don't control the way we think or run our lives. We've got to limit working for a situation that's other than ours. We have no ownership of anything. If you don't own business, then you don't have jobs. White people have jobs because they have business. They have institutions that teach them how to live in America. Black people don't have institutions that teach them how to deal with s - t. The Number One institution that teaches you how to deal is the family, but slavery f - ked that up. So the song is about the ongoing cost of the holocaust. There was a Jewish holocaust, but there's a black holocaust that people still choose to ignore.[14]

13) www.youtube.com/watch?v=am9BqZ6eA5c

14) genius.com/Public-enemy-cant-truss-it-lyrics. The *Genius.com* website gives the lyrics of many popular songs and poems with notes to help in understanding. It is a valuable website for anyone interested in popular music.

Q : Find the lyrics to "Can't Truss It" and see if you need help in understanding any of them.

One of the greatest rappers of the 90s was Tupac Shakur (or 2Pac), a west-coast rapper. He rapped about the "gangsta" life, but he also turned toward more socially conscious lyrics. He had a string of hits in the 90s, including "Only God Can Judge Me" (1995)[15] and "Dear Mama" (1995).[16] The first song shows his criminal background and presents it as a means of survival. The second song pays homage to his mother for trying to raise him well in the face of many difficulties. In 1996, he released "2 of Amerikaz Most Wanted" with Snoop Dogg,[17] another well-known rapper.[18] Sadly, Tupac was shot and killed in Las Vegas in 1996, a victim of his own "gangsta" youth. He did make a recent posthumous public appearance with Snoop Dogg at Coachella, an annual popular music festival in California. In 2012, he appeared as a hologram on stage.[19]

Q : Find the lyrics to "Only God Can Judge Me," "Dear Mama," and "2 of Amerikaz Most Wanted," and

15) www.youtube.com/watch?v=rh9S4vLDDOI

16) www.youtube.com/watch?v=Mb1ZvUDvLDY

17) www.youtube.com/watch?v=BL6dWDfs5x8

18) Some people might know him from the video he made with Korea's Psy, "Hangover" (2014), a video about Korea's drinking culture.

19) www.youtube.com/watch?v=TGbrFmPBV0Y

see if you need help in understanding any of them.

In 1993, Queen Latifah came out with "UNITY."[20] She protests against the sexism of the kind that is found in songs like "Straight Outta Compton," as well as in real life. In "UNITY," she sends a shout-out to Aretha Franklin. In the 60s, Aretha spelled out her call for men to treat women with "R-E-S-P-E-C-T." Queen Latifah likewise spells out her call for women to come together in opposing sexism: "U-N-I-T-Y." Latifah has many talents, and she went on to become a film star. She is one of the most influential women in entertainment today.

Q : Find the lyrics to "U-N-I-T-Y" and see if you need help in understanding any of them.

Throughout the 90s, women artists had a significant effect on America's listening habits. Some of those artists wrote out of social awareness. For instance, Melissa Etheridge's 1994 "Come to My Window" might seem like a conventional love song with these lines: "I don't care what they think. / I don't care what they say. / What do they know about this love anyway?"[21] Many listeners might hear a reference to a young, Romeo-and-Juliette kind of forbidden love. People

20) www.youtube.com/watch?v=f8cHxydDb7o&feature=related

21) www.youtube.com/watch?v=5EGx4_WSMSE&feature=channel

who are aware of Etheridge's sexual orientation and involvement with the LGBTQ communities understand those lyrics as including a reference to same-sex love, however.

Q : Find the lyrics to "Come to My Window" and see if you need help in understanding any of them.

As always, other pop singers showed little concern for social issues and released music that focused on the self. A woman singer who took the pop world by storm with such music was Britney Spears, who exploded onto the scene with her 1998 hit, "(Hit Me) Baby One More Time." That seemed to initiate a time in which women became in many ways the most recognizable people in pop music, many combining intricate choreography with music in their videos, prefiguring the rise of k-pop, an eclectic form of popular music that gathers influences for its own manufactured creativity.

Some of the women who have followed Britney and the older Madonna in becoming important pop music stars in the 21st-century are Beyoncé, Lady Gaga, Nicki Minaj, and Taylor Swift. Neither of the latter two show much social consciousness. Taylor Swift, who moved from the country to the pop charts, seems to be most famous for singing about her own romantic indulgences. Nicki Minaj, a rapper, is likewise self-indulgent in her sometime pre-occupation with her own sexuality. Like much of modern rap, Minaj's

"Anaconda" (2014) and "Only" (2015) focus on the superiority of the rapper, in sexuality, rapping ability, and wealth, celebrating the individual rather than any community or social consciousness.

I am sure most readers will have favorite contemporary musical artists that they might want to include in this survey. I encourage taking some time in class through group presentations or discussions, to explore the significance of those artists, as well as other artists from the past that continue to influence today's music. There are many other musical artists that could be included here, but I will finish with one who may not be the most well-known but who shows how rap has become one of the most significant musical modes of the contemporary world. As noted above, rap and hip-hop culture have spread throughout the world and been adapted to individual local and national cultures.

One of the most interesting adaptations of rap is in communities of the original Americans: Indians, Native Americans, first nations' peoples. An online exploration of those rappers shows many creative artists. One of those who carries forward the early social concerns of rap music and turns it toward his own people is an artist known as Supaman. Besides being a rapper, he is also a champion fancy dancer. Fancy dancing is a style of dance developed from the original folk forms of dance in Native American cultures. The dancers wear elaborate costumes and dance with great energy.

In "Prayer Loop Song" (2014), Supaman wears his fancy-dance attire (clothes) and blends Native rhythms and instruments with rap rhythms and the hip-hop technique of layering sound through looping, a repetition of accumulated recorded sounds.[22] The words of his song layer on yet another tradition, that of Christianity. Supaman's song thus becomes a representation of America at its best, with multiple cultures blended in one hopeful music.

Q : Find the lyrics to "Prayer Loop Song" and see if you need help in understanding any of them.

Throughout this overview of American popular music, and throughout this book, students have been urged to find things on the internet. The technological innovations of the 21st century have enabled us to listen to our music almost anywhere, and those innovations, technological and otherwise, have influenced many facets of our lives. Early in the century, in 2002, "American Idol" began its run on television. There are now idol-type shows in most countries throughout the world. Indeed, "American Idol" was originally a copy of a British television show.

In 2001, the ipod was first sold. This was a great improvement over the Walkman and similar portable CD players because the music could be digitally stored so that people did not need to carry their cassettes or CDs with them in order to listen to music. Of course, systems like the iphone (2007) and Android (2008) made it possible to

22) www.youtube.com/watch?v=_0jq7jIa34Y

load that music onto your phone so that one device could serve the purpose of two. The wide availability of smart phones has now let us bring the internet almost everywhere we go. At one time, people were tied to a fixed physical location while using the internet. Not anymore. We don't even need to load music onto our devices; we can store it in the "cloud." Or we can open one of the online music service like *Youtube* or *Vimeo* on our smart phones.

21st-century connectivity has also seen the development of vast social networks like Linked In (started in 2003), Facebook (2004), Twitter (2006), Instagram (2010), Kakaotalk (2010), Pinterest (2010), and Snapchat (2011). We can now use multiple applications to communicate almost instantaneously with people throughout the world. When I first came to Korea in the 1980s, I communicated with friends and family in the U.S. almost entirely by writing letters on paper and sending them through the postal service as "snail mail." Now, I can have a face-to-face chat with those friends and family using a smart phone application while I am sitting in a Korean coffee shop. The latest developments in American popular culture are at our fingertips, so there is virtually no delay between their introduction in America and our ability to know about them in Korea.

FOR FURTHER CONSIDERATION

Discuss the ways in which the lyrics to "Thunder

Road," "Born to Run," and/or "Stayin' Alive" address the challenges and frustrations of blue-collar, working class life.

Watch the video and follow the lyrics of "Can't Truss It." The video tells two stories, one from the past, and one from the present. Discuss the ways in which the two stories parallel one another. Also, consider ways that the lyrics match the stories.

Beyoncé and Lady Gaga certainly show some self-indulgences, but they also have created music that speaks to larger social issues and to empowering their listeners, especially young women. Consider Beyoncé's "Girls (Who Run the World)"[23] and Gaga's "Born this Way,"[24] both from 2011, for how they may or may not give messages of empowerment to women listeners.

For a cross-cultural exploration, compare Beyoncé's "Girls (Who Run the World)" with Brown-Eyed Girls' "Sixth Sense,"[25] both from 2011.

Another interesting cross-cultural comparison would be to consider the images of Wonder Woman, a famous American

23) www.youtube.com/watch?v=VBmMU_iwe6U

24) www.youtube.com/watch?v=wV1FrqwZyKw

25) www.youtube.com/watch?v=pIqkDBsSJOw

comic book, television, and movie hero in three music videos, two Korean and one American: Wonder Girls' "Tell Me" (2007),[26] G-Dragon's "Crayon" (2013),[27] and Lady Gaga's and Beyoncé's "Telephone" (2009).[28] Consider whether or not the videos give positive images for young women viewers. William Marston, who created Wonder Woman as a comic-book hero in 1941, "aimed, with his tales, at a male audience, men or boys whom he hoped would embrace his doctrine of male submission to superior, loving females."[29]

Find all of the American pop culture references in G-Dragon's music video "Crayon."

For ways in which contemporary pop music can challenge listeners with political messages, consider two songs by Beyoncé: "Formation"[30] and "Hold Up"[31] (both 2016). Listen to the songs, try to understand them as well as you can, watch the music videos, and research the controversies about the songs.[32]

---

26) www.youtube.com/watch?v=BlHv3BbBv6A

27) www.youtube.com/watch?v=t3ULhmadHkg&list=PL0D12C278EAF39032

28) www.youtube.com/watch?v=EVBsypHzF3U

29) Stanley, Kellie. "'Suffering Sappho!': Wonder Woman and the (Re) Invention of the Feminine Ideal." *Helios* 32.2 (2005): 143-171. (149)

30) www.youtube.com/watch?v=WDZJPJV__bQ

31) www.youtube.com/watch?v=PeonBmeFR8o

32) The analysis of the songs at *Genius.com* will be helpful, but internet searches of, for example, "Beyoncé Formation controversy" will also give you many insights into songs and their reception.

Topic 18

The Movies and American Popular Culture

When we think about American popular culture as an export, movies come to mind immediately as one of the most obvious cultural artifacts that are distributed throughout the world. Like music, movies reflect the times in which they are made. Take the 2014 film *Selma*, for instance. It is a film that focuses on a series of Civil Rights actions that took place on the Edmund Pettus Bridge in Selma, Alabama in 1965. Those actions helped lead to the passage of the 1965 Voting Rights Act that made it illegal for individual states to prevent black citizens from voting. When a film like *Selma* is made, we see it as a way of showing younger viewers something about American history, but, just as important, we see a comment on a temporary American culture in which racial differences remain an issue.

One of the very first silent-movie hits blended politics and film. In 1915, *The Birth of a Nation* gave a positive, heroic depiction of the rise of the KKK (Ku Klux Klan), a group dedicated to white supremacy. That film honored the people who created the legal systems that prevented black citizens from exercising their right to vote. In 2016, a film of the same name, *The Birth of a Nation*, depicted the 1831 slave revolt led by Nat Turner in a heroic fashion. In that revolt, a group of slaves attempted to march on Richmond,

Virginia, killing many white people along the way.

Selma and *Birth of a Nation* are both produced with an intentional and overt political message. Other films, like many light comedies or romances, do not have an intentional political stance but can be analyzed through a political lens. For one obvious example, films that present women as sexual objects can be analyzed through a feminist lens. Films that show a violent "rugged individual," no matter how righteous his cause, might be critiqued for overly violent images. Films that glamorize wealthy people might be critiqued for accepting a world of economic inequality. Conversely, films might be praised for having a protagonist who shows the flaws of ordinary people but is embraced even with those flaws. A science fiction film about overcoming an evil empire might be read as a reflection on contemporary situations in the world, from either a liberal or a conservative perspective, and, perhap, even from both.

Q : What is a recent American movie you have seen? Do you think it has a politics to it?

A film also might be considered for purely aesthetic principles like complex storytelling, intricate and intelligent camera angles, pacing, and dialogue. Whatever approach one might take, good films are open to multiple revelations about the way people think about the world.

Film study also shows connections of the past with

the present, as in the juxtapostiion of the two films titled *The Birth of a Nation.* Film critic Philip French outlines the history of American film through the first decade of the 21st century like this:[1)]

1910-1919: The birth of Hollywood
1920-1929: The advent of sound
1930-1939: The age of Technicolor
1940-1949: The movies go to war
1950-1959: The battle with television
1960-1969: The European threat
1970-1979: Hollywood strikes back
1980-1989: The suits regain control
1990-1999: Animation makes a comeback
2000-2009: A sense of déjà-vu

While French's decade-by-decade division reflects his own personal taste, it also shows that films are influenced by the times in which they are made.

The 20th century saw the rise and fall of film as a primary means of entertainment. As we can see from French's list, television became a major competitor for movies in the 1950s. Technological developments in using the television for playing movies rather than watching network programs helped revive the movie industry. Beginning in the 1970s, people could rent movies on tape to play on a mchine

1) "How 100 Years of Hollywood Have Charted the History of America." *The Guardian* 28 Feb. 2010. https://www.theguardian.com/film/2010/feb/28/philip-french-best-hollywood-films

connected to their televisions. In the 1990s, DVD (Digital Video Disc) technology was perfected, and customers could go to a video store to rent movies or order them from a DVD-delivery service like Netflix. Now, most people watch movies at home through a video-streaming service. Netflix, for instance, has evolved into such a service, and it has expanded globally, arriving in South Korea in 2016.

These days, going out to the movies is still a popular pasttime for family fun as well as for dating. While the sizes of television screens have increased dramatically in the last twenty years, those screens cannot replicate the sensual experience of a movie theater.

In the next two chapters, we will look at two relatively recent films to consider how films reflect social and political contexts. The first is one of the highest grossing films of all time, the 2009 *Avatar*.[2] The second is a recent film version of a classic American novel, *The Great Gatsby*, from 2013, the most recent of five movie versions of F. Scott Fitzgerald's 1925 novel.

FOR FURTHER CONSIDERATION

Find a website that lists the nominees and winners of the most recent Academy Awards (the Oscars), especially for Best Picture. How many of the films on that list have

2) The "gross" refers to total box office receipts, how much people paid for tickets to the movie. It is a good measure for the popularity of a film.

you seen? Which did you think were the best? Why?

If you have not seen any of the Oscar-nominated movies or have seen only one or two, which of the others would you like to watch? Why?

Why are the Academy Awards called the Oscars? Try to find out the answer.

What is your favorite American movie? Why?

What American movies are currently playing in nearby theaters? Which would you most like to see? Why?

Learn about and present the history of home movie entertainment to the class.

What is your favorite movie ever? Tell us why.

Topic 19

Re-Imagining Exceptionalism in the Movies — *Avatar*

Avatar was admired for its complex and stunning use of CGI (Computer-Generated Imagery) to create a world of natural beauty and wonder. There is perhaps some irony in a movie that celebrates the environment and getting back to nature at the same time as it uses the most advanced technologies for movie making.

Rather than spend very much space describing the movie, this chapter starts with one assignment: watch the movie (perhaps together as a class), using English subtitles to help you follow the dialogue, and ask the instructor about anything you do not understand.

After completing that assignment, read the topics for further consideration, follow the directions, and watch the movie one more time. The second time you watch the movie, you should stop it from time to time to analyze the scenes, action, and themes.

Finally, discuss the film in class or submit written responses to the film, guided by the further considerations.

FOR FURTHER CONSIDERATION

Consider the different ways in which Jake Sully is depicted as an almost god-like individual.

Early in *Avatar*, Jake Sully in his avatar body on his first experience in the forest becomes separated from his companions. While he is wandering in the forest, one of the camera angles is from above him, in the trees. This perspective puts the viewer in the position of the Na'vi. Consider the ramifications of this perspective for the viewer. You might recall the consideration of women in advertising in Chapter 10, and how the viewer, whether male or female, is put into the masculine position by looking through the male "gaze." In both of those instances, we can see how choices of visual perspective influence interpretation and understanding.

Search the internet for *Avatar* fan sites and report back to the class on what you find.

Below is information about eight different reactions to *Avatar*. Select one of these opinion that seems interesting to you, look at the full essay, and consider how the writer's perspective on the film compares to your own perspective.

Davidson, Rjurik. "Evaluating a Film in a World of

Its Own." *Screen Education* 57 (Autumn 2010): 10-17.

Keegan, Rebecca. "James Cameron: Closet Feminist." *Vanity Fair* 15 December 2009.[1]

Marlowe, Ann. "The Most Neo-Con Movie Ever Made." *Forbes* 23 December 2009.[2]

Meade, Frederick Alexander. "Avatar: An Extension of White Supremacy." *Countercurrents* 5 January 2010.[3]

Newitz, Annalee. "When Will White People Stop Making Movies Like 'Avatar'?" *io9.com* 18 December 2009.[4]

Podhoretz, John. "Avatrocious." *The Weekly Standard* 15.15 (28 December 2009).[5]

Yoon, Carol Kaesuk. "Luminous 3-D Jungle Is a Biologist's Dream." *NY Times* 19 January 2010.[6]

Zizek, Slavoj. "Return of the Natives." *New Statesman* 4 March 2010.[7]

1) www.vanityfair.com/online/oscars/2009/12/james-cameron-closet-feminist
2) www.forbes.com/2009/12/23/avatar-neo-con-military-opinions-contributors-ann-marlowe.html
3) www.countercurrents.org/meade050110.htm
4) io9.com/5422666/when-will-white-people-stop-making-movies-like avatar
5) www.weeklystandard.com/avatarocious/article/272354
6) www.nytimes.com/2010/01/19/science/19essay.html
7) www.newstatesman.com/film/2010/03/avatar-reality-love-couple-sex

Topic 20

The Past in the Present in the Movies – *The Great Gastby*

The Great Gatsby, like much of the popular culture we have discussed, connects the past to the present. As many of the critics below recognize, that connection is made through music in this film. Another significant connection is that this film is an adaptation of F. Scott Fitzgerald's 1925 classic of American literature, the novel with the same title as the movie. This novel gives one of the most famous depictions of the American character. As you watch the movie, think about how it might reflect some of the American ideas, characteristics, and beliefs that we have studied. You will note that Tom Buchannan, for instance, expresses some very American ideas about race, seeing black people as inferior to white people. The audience should not agree with his opinions, so that the film expresses support for American diversity at the same time as it shows that not all Americans accept the idea. That should remind you of the very first chapter of the book, suggesting that the present, even in the pages of this book, has its roots in the past.

As in the previous chapter, rather than spend very much space describing the movie, this chapter starts with one assignment: watch the movie (perhaps together as a class), using English subtitles to help you follow the dialogue, and ask the instructor about anything you do not understand.

After completing that assignment, read the topics for further consideration, follow the directions, and watch the movie one more time. The second time you watch the movie, you should stop it from time to time to analyze the scenes, action, and themes.

Finally, discuss the film in class or submit written responses to the film, guided by the further considerations.

FOR FURTHER CONSIDERATION

Besides the hip-hop soundtrack, how do you think the world of *The Great Gatsby* is similar to or different from our own time? Please use specific examples.

When Nick and Gatsby first drive into the city, they pass a group of people in a car on a bridge. Describe this scene and how it might be important to the film.

At one point early in the film, Daisy is in a room with the windows open and the curtains blowing freely in the wind. Tom enters the room and closes the windows. Discuss how this scene reveals the characters of Tom and Daisy, and what it suggests about their relationship.

Below is information about several different reactions to *The Great Gatsby*. Select two of these that seem to offer opposing viewpoints, look at the full essays, and explain which one you think gives a more insightful perspective on the movie.

Allison. "*The Great Gatsby* Proves the Timelessness of Hip Hop." *Film School Rejects* 16 May 2013.[1)]

Bassil, Ryan. "Who Let *The Great Gatsby* Soundtrack Happen?" Noisey 16 May 2013.[2)]

Bradley, Reginia N. "Fade to Black, Old Sport: How Hip Hop Amplifies Baz Luhrmann's *The Great Gatsby*." *Sounding Out!* 21 October 2013.[3)]

Denby, David. "All That Jazz: *The Great Gatsby*." *The New Yorker* 13 May 2013.[4)]

French, Philip. "*The Great Gatsby*: Review." *The Guardian* 18 May 2013.[5)]

Giardina, Carolyn. "Why *The Great Gatsby* May Be the Most Influential Film of 2013." *The Hollywood Reporter* 14 January 2014.[6)]

1) filmschoolrejects.com/the-great-gatsby-proves-the-timelessness-of-hip-hop-6cb75a8cd33f#.te06x3uhu

2) noisey.vice.com/en_uk/article/who-let-the-great-gatsby-soundtrack-happen

3) soundstudiesblog.com/2013/10/21/fade-to-black-old-sport-how-hip-hop-amplifies-baz-luhrmanns-the-great-gatsby/

4) www.newyorker.com/magazine/2013/05/13/all-that-jazz-3

5) www.theguardian.com/film/2013/may/19/great-gatsby-review-philip-french

6) www.hollywoodreporter.com/news/why-great-gatsby-may-be-670661

Graham, Jane. "*The Great Gatsby*: A Hip-Hop State of Mind." *The Big Issue* 12 June 2013.[7]

Lefebvre, Sam. "*The Great Gatsby's* Soundtrack Doesn't Fit Its Message." *SF Weekly* 22 May 2013.[8]

Moore, Charles. "Baz Luhrmann's *The Great Gatsby*: A Faithful Film – And a Terribly, Terribly Bad One." *The Telegraph* 19 May, 2013.[9]

7) www.bigissue.com/features/2533/great-gatsby-hip-hop-state-mind

8) archives.sfweekly.com/sanfrancisco/the-great-gatsbys-soundtrack-doesnt-fit-its-message/Content?oid=2825985

9) www.telegraph.co.uk/culture/film/filmreviews/10067605/Baz-Luhrmanns-The-Great-Gatsby-a-faithful-film-and-a-terribly-terribly-bad-one.html